I0482551

ZenDoodle Underwater World!

Learning to draw Amazing Zen and Doodle Pictures

By Veronica Kim

Table of Contents

Disclaimer

While all attempts have been made to verify the information provided in this book, the author does assume any responsibility for errors, omissions, or contrary interpretations of the subject matter contained within. **The information provided in this book is for educational and entertainment purposes only. The reader is responsible for his or her own actions and the author does not accept any responsibilities for any liabilities or damages, real or perceived, resulting from the use of this information.**

The trademarks that are used are without any consent, and the publication of the trademark is without permission or backing by the trademark owner. All trademarks and brands within this book are for clarifying purposes only and are the owned by the owners themselves, not affiliated with this document.

Introduction

Individuals are once in a while mindful of the way that we are a nature's piece. We get lost effectively in this aggressive life and overlook that we have to return to the nature as a wellspring of peace and our presence. No one but nature can take us back to our roots. That is the reason, every one of us, now and again, need to encounter what nature brings to the table. That will give us the quality we have to proceed.

When I say, where everything started, I mean ocean. It is astounding how intense it is the point at which you simply consider how immense it is and what it covers up. In the event that you are overcome enough to dive deep down to investigate than you ought to do it, most likely. What you will feel and experience you can't discover on Discovery Channel. Nonetheless, in the event that you are not genuine darling of the profundity and the dimness of the underwater world, why would it be advisable for you to miss on the experience when considerably prettier pictures you can find in the few meters profundity?

Entrancing underwater world offer you a lot of vivid plants, wipes and fishes swimming among the coral reefs and will abandon you with feeling, as you were simply a piece of something unnatural. Climate you are proficient or unpracticed jumper you will be totally lured. It is only that, on the off chance that it is you're first or second time, and you were pondering how you will do it, do it again keeping in mind the end goal to have an opportunity to experience this underwater scene more casual and dread free.

Such a variety of destinations in our valuable world can offer this sort of good times for you. On the off chance that you have nobody near you that can prescribe a specific destination from their experience, contact your travel specialists, let him know what precisely you had at the top of the priority list, book all that you have to book and keep in mind your waterproof camera on the grounds that you without a doubt need to catch what you speak the truth to encounter.

Chapter 1 – How to draw fish

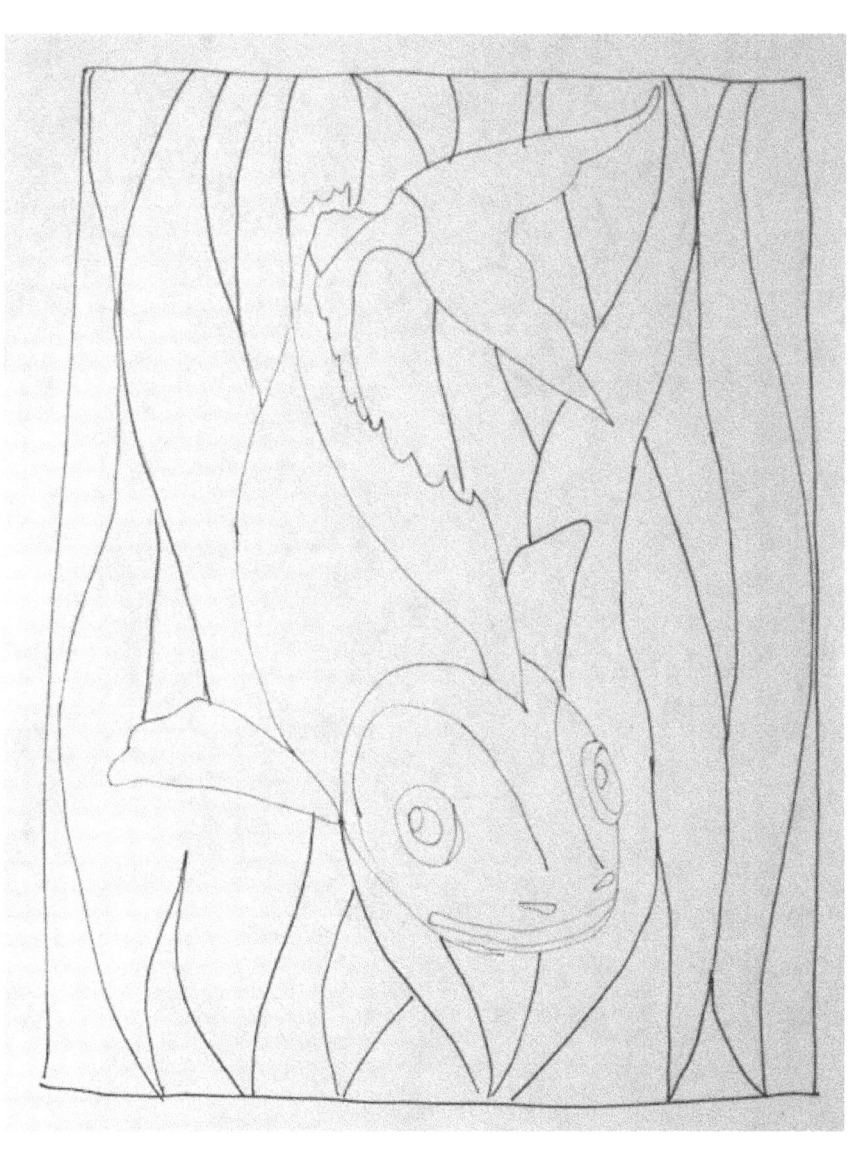

Step 1: Start with a basic circle amidst your paper.

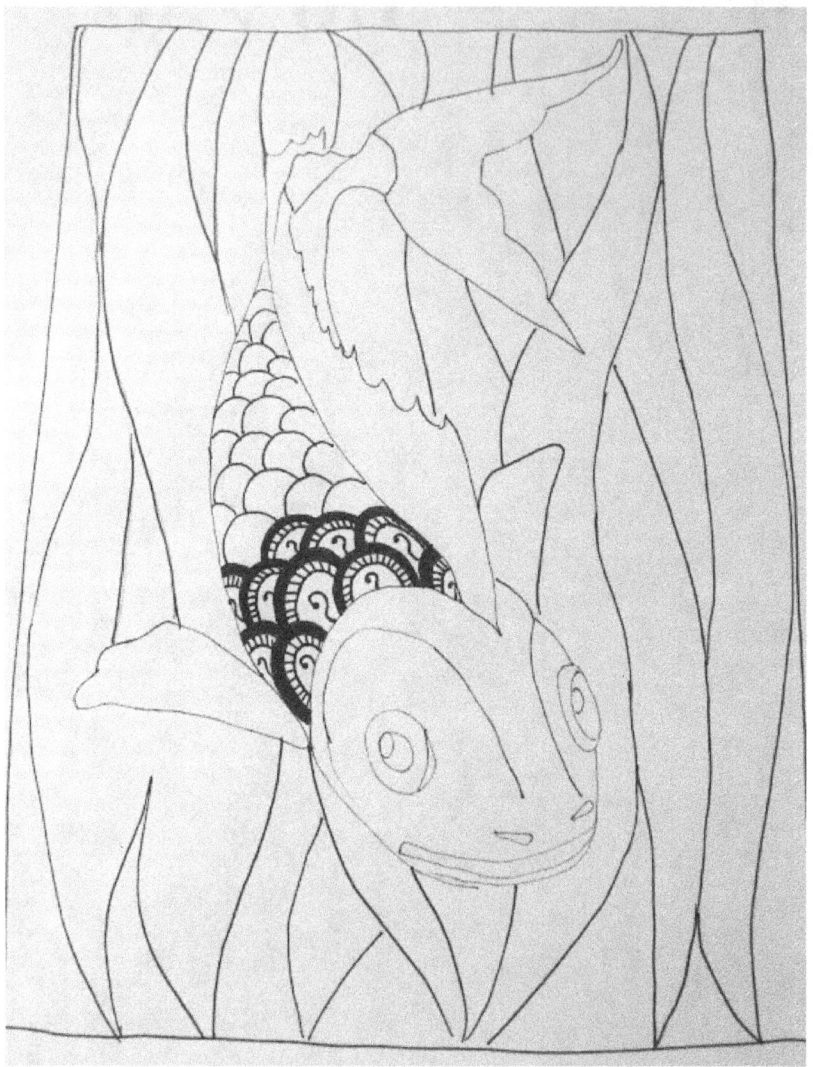

Step 2: Draw a bended line inside the circle.

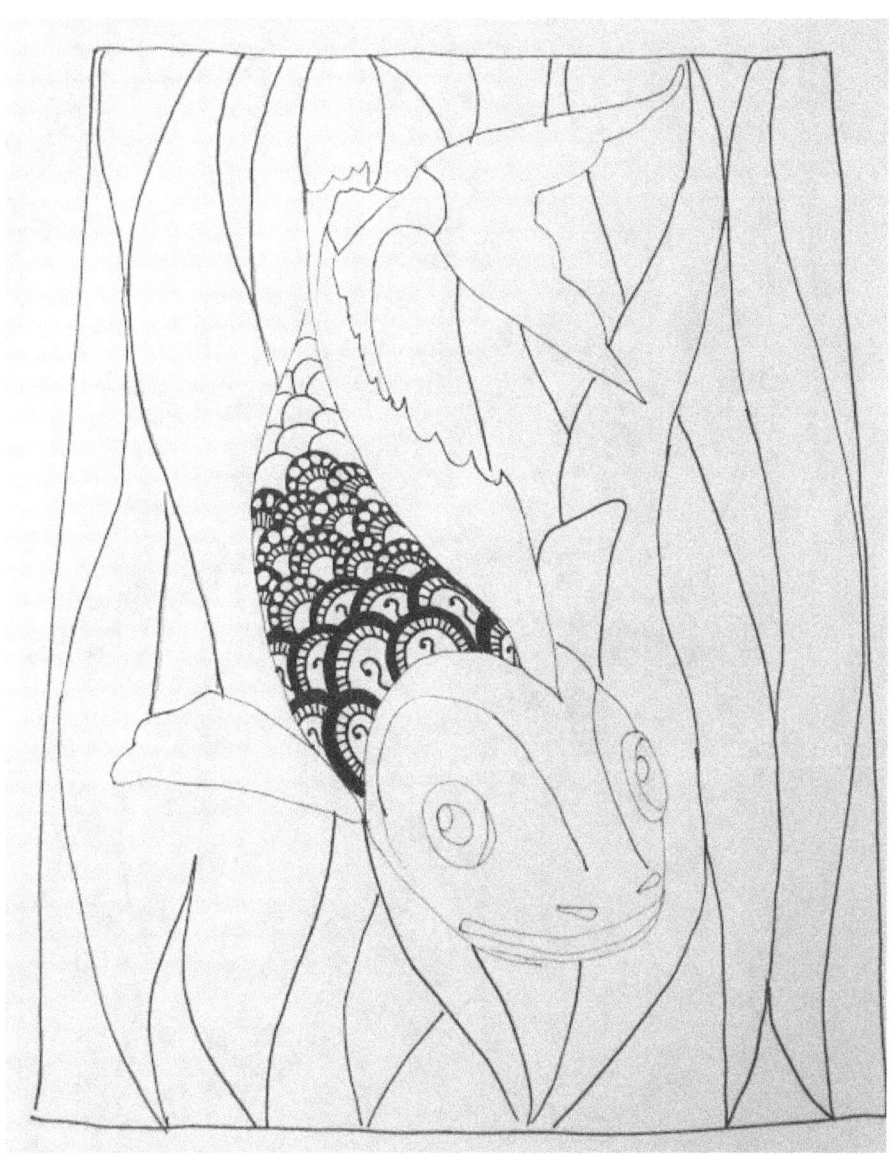

Step 3: Add two littler bended lines to one side of the greater one. These speak to the gills. At that point, include an energized eye.

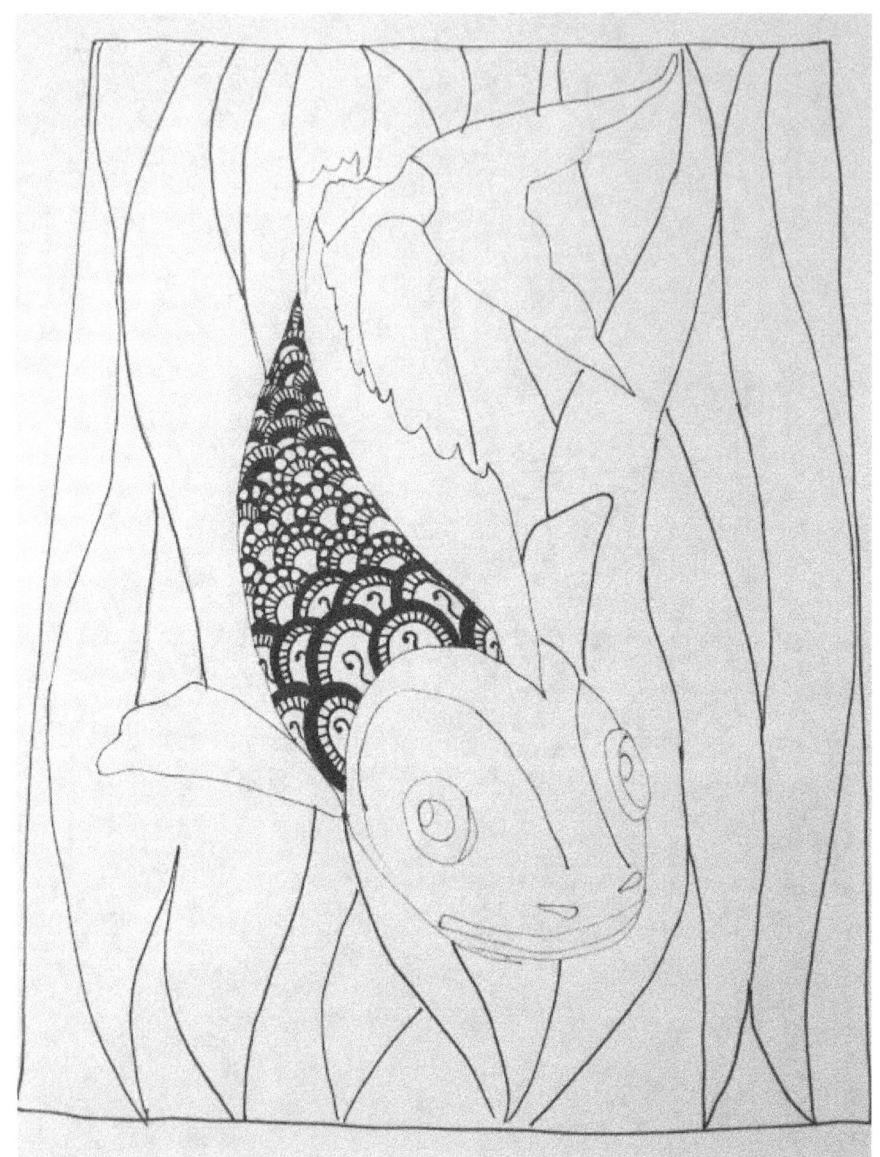

Step 4: Draw stout lips utilizing covering bended lines. At that point, draw medium measured scales utilizing the same covering bended lines. It's valuable to do this in columns.

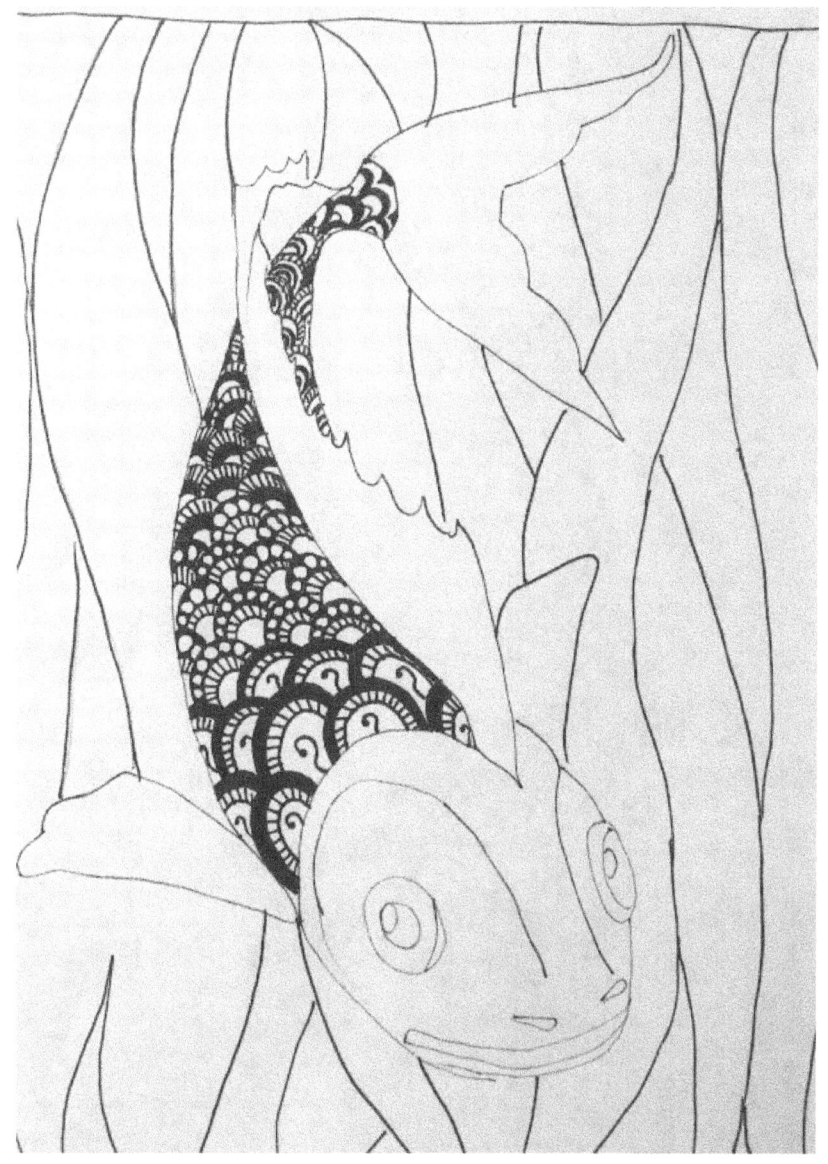

Step 5: Draw two tail balances and a top blade. For the back fins, these ought to be sideways raindrop shapes.

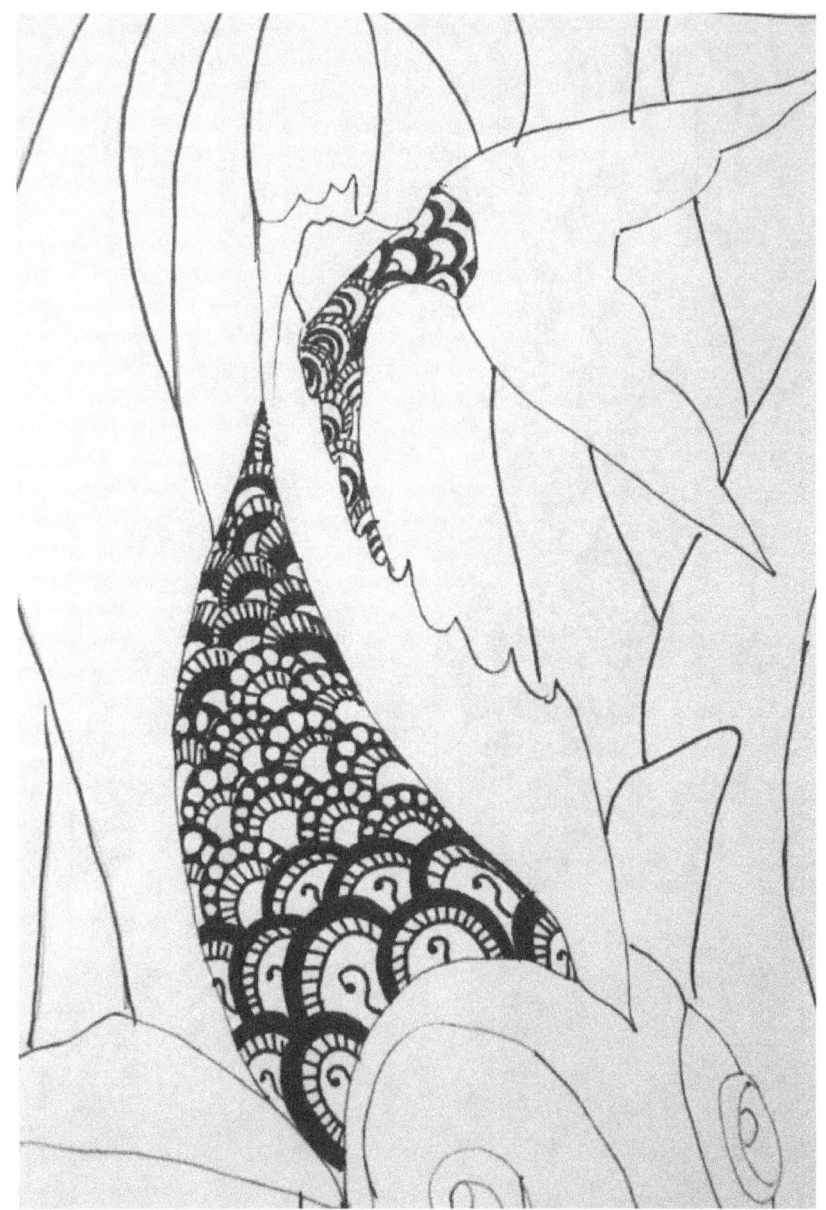

Step 6: Draw bended lines within them to give them surface. At that point, include a darker line between each of those back balances to demonstrate that there are two balances. For the top blade, utilize a half raindrop shape. Include any line outline you need within this shape!

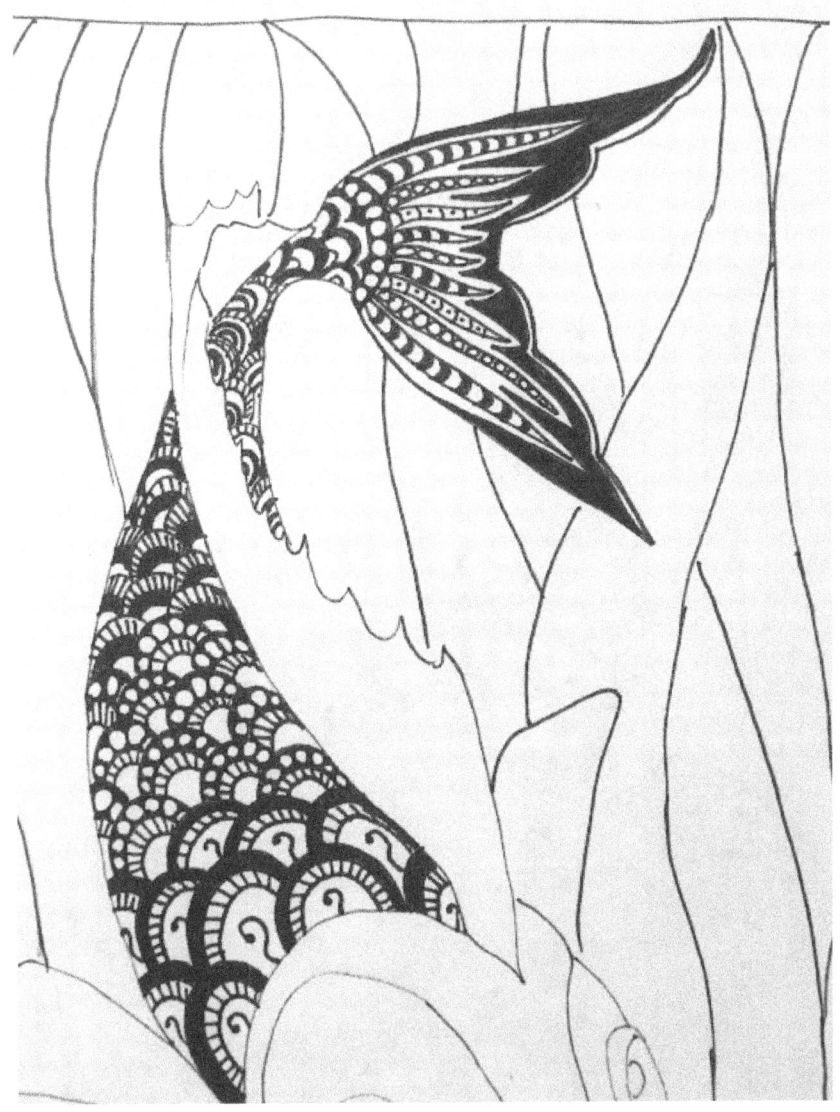

Step 7: Add two longer base fins utilizing the same shape just making them skinnier and more. Add little dashes and lines to include surface.

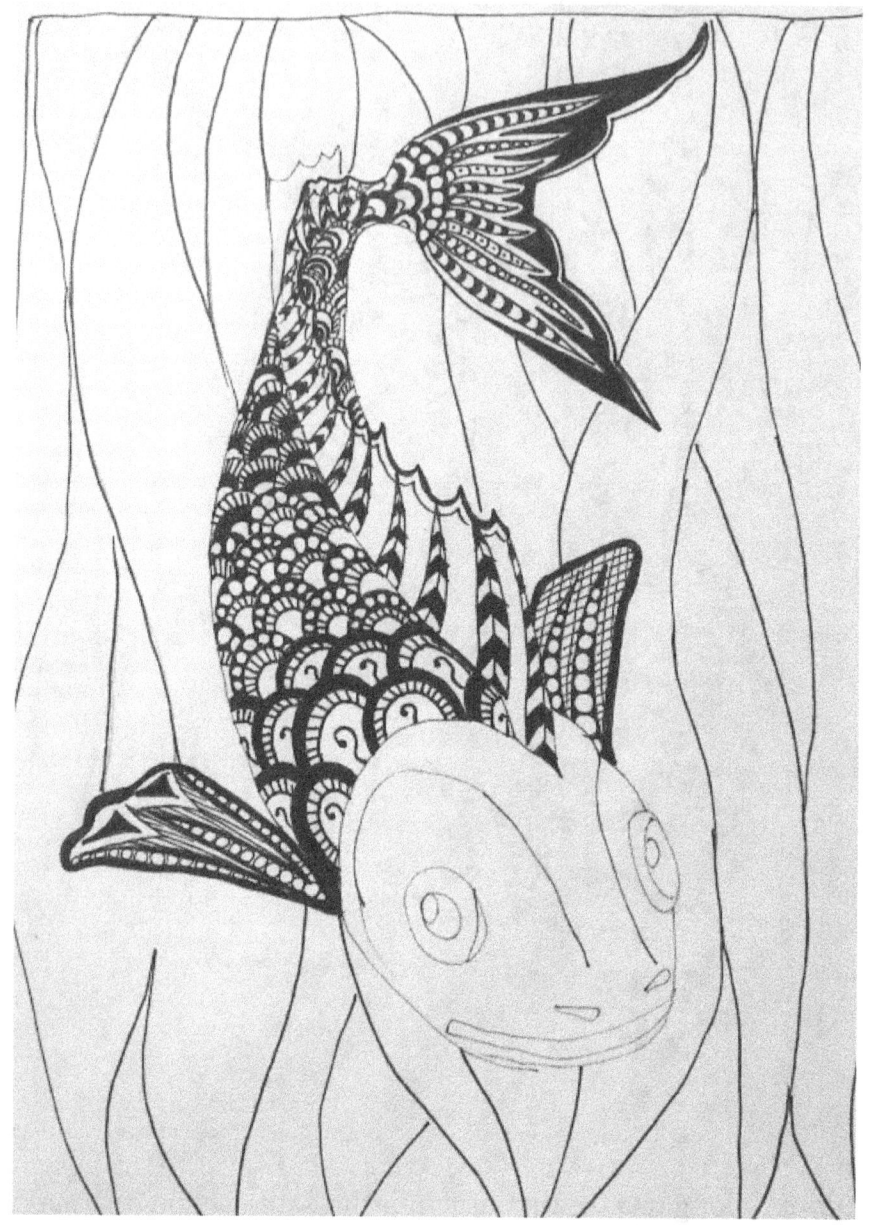

Step 8: Once you're done, include whatever other little subtle elements, for example, more compositions to the fins.

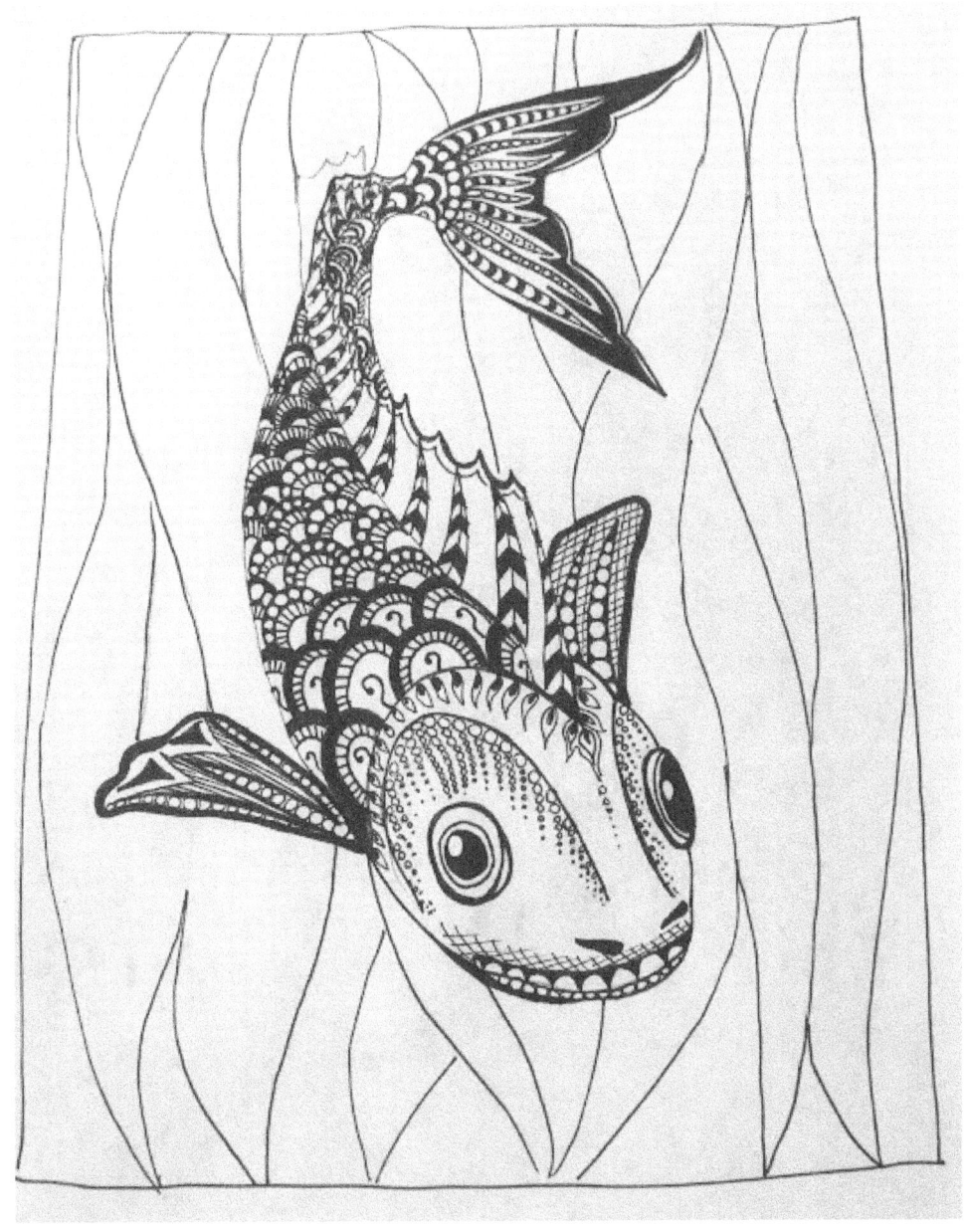

Step 9: As you can see we have worked on the eyes and face area in this figure.

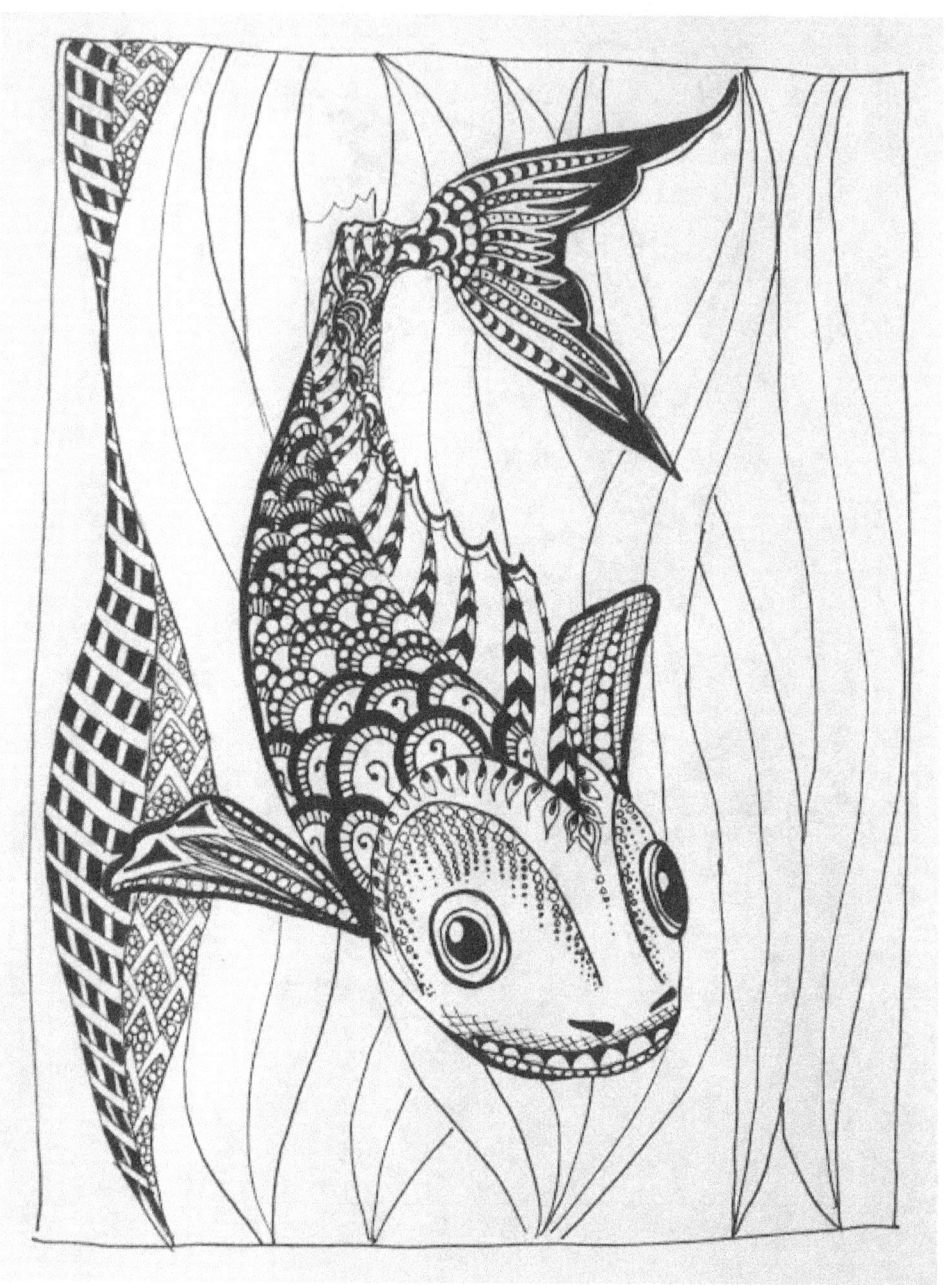

Step 10: We have now started working on the grass area with the shading to give it a better and appropriate details.

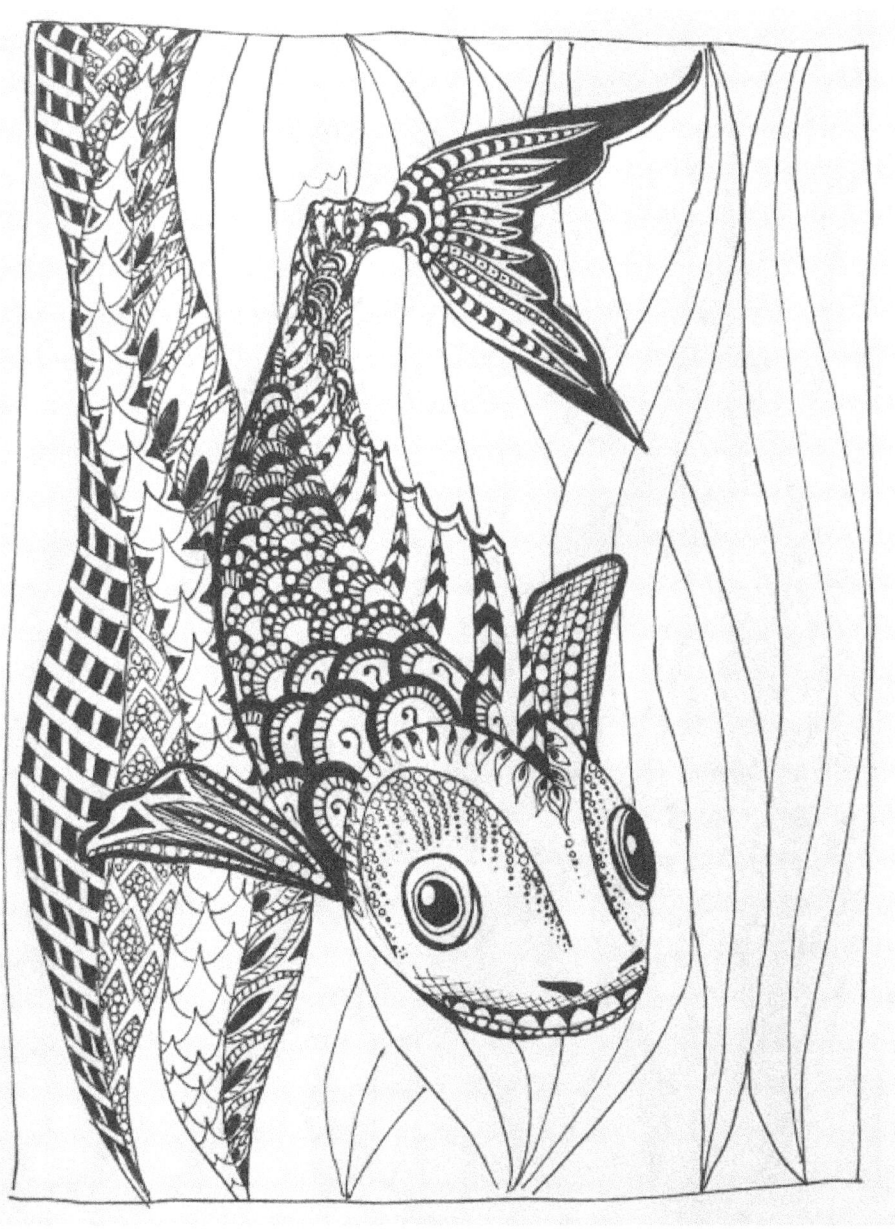

Step 11: Here we have worked on the 2nd area of the underwater grass which we drew with lines in the starting.

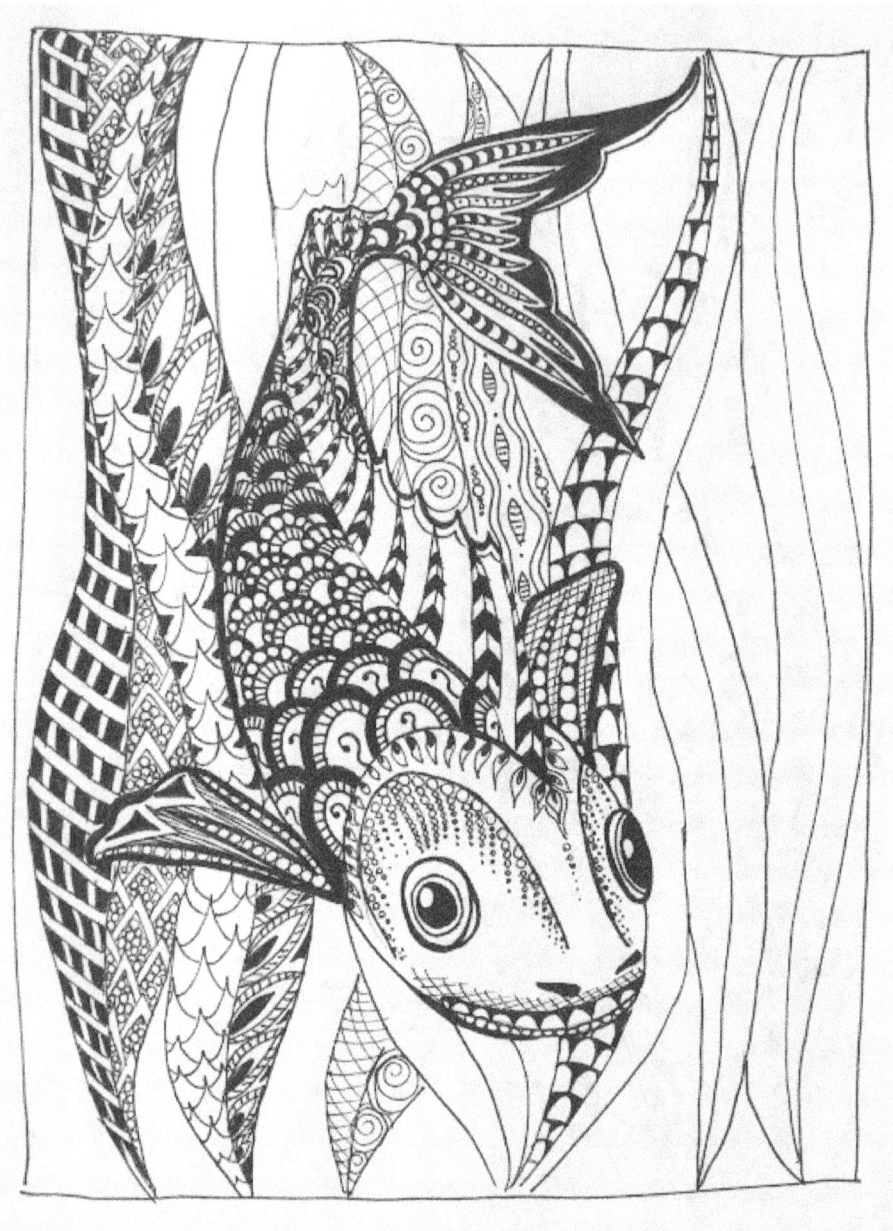

Step 12: Drawing the underwater grass and shading it has given this fish a new look.

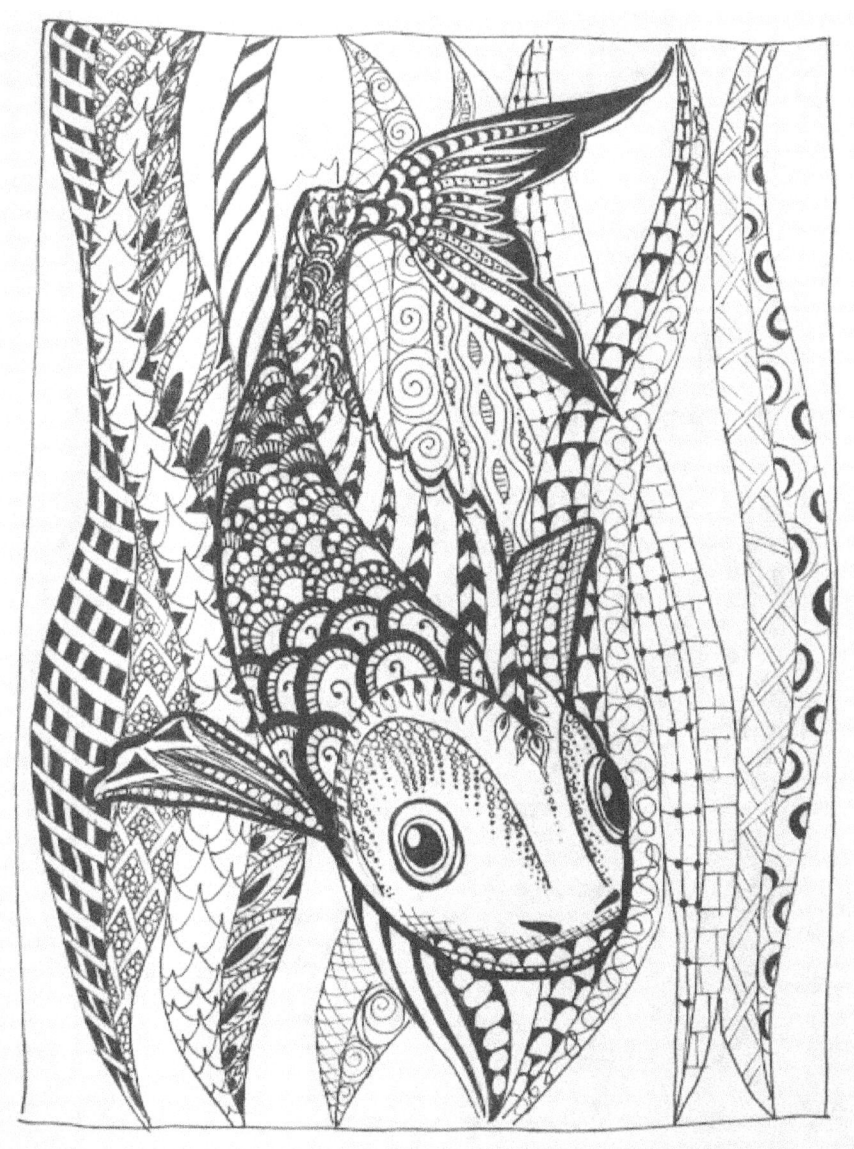

Step 13: At this step, we are almost close to be done; with giving the underwater different types of shading we have given this fish a bright look.

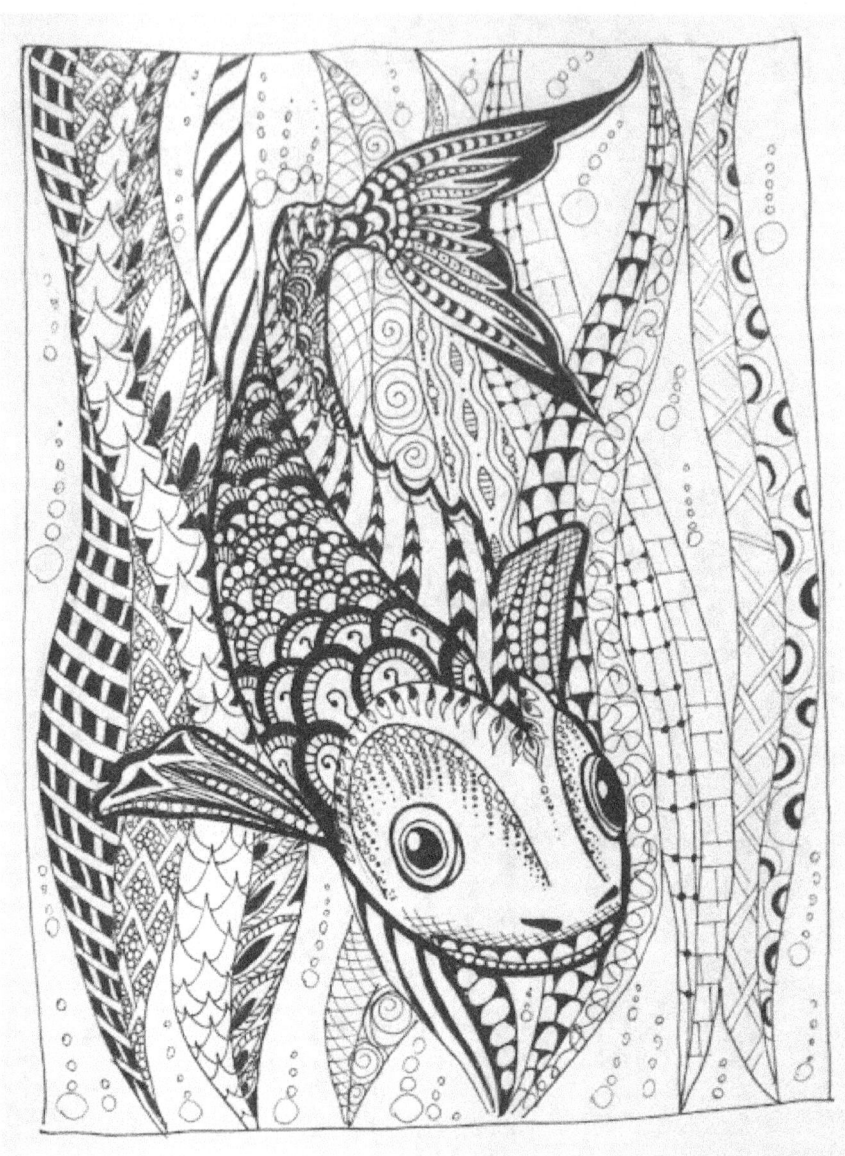

Step 14: With the water bubbles in different sizes we have shown that the fish is underwater and the water has different impact on the grass. More like it's moving in the water.

Chapter 2 – How to draw fish

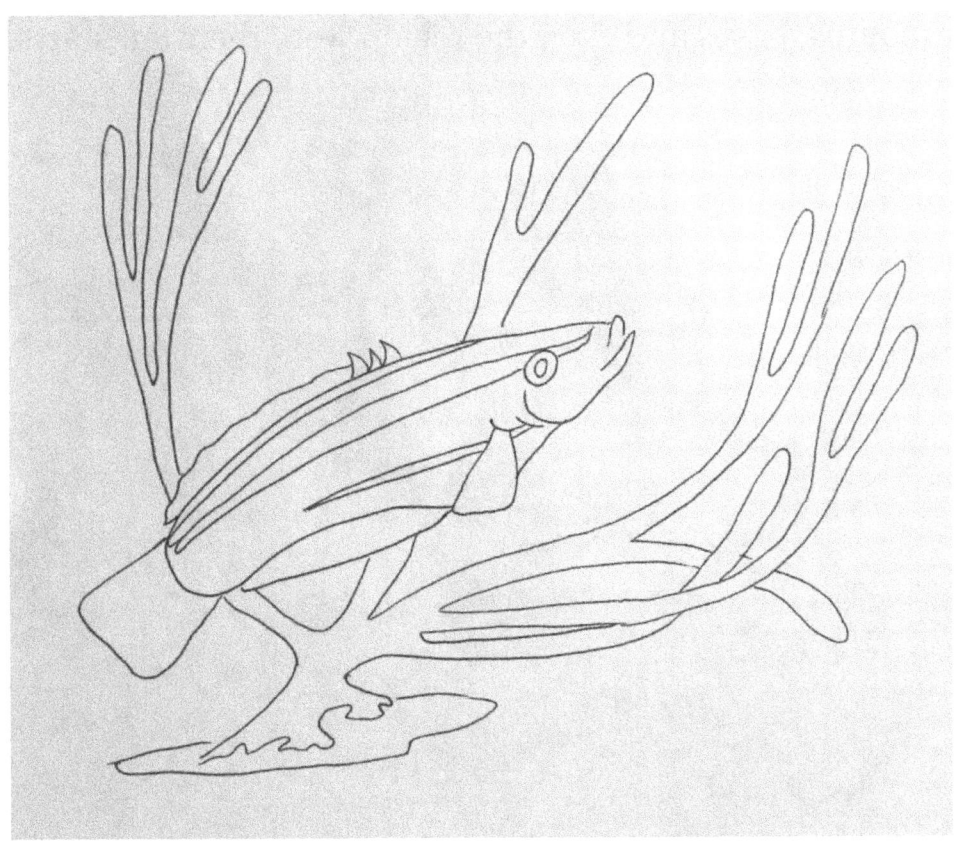

Step 1: Start by drawing various types of body shapes. To begin with, draw a contorted oval shape with a substantial knock beneath it, a heart shape body for the second fish, a pointed oval shape for the third shape and afterward at long last an adjusted square for the fourth tropical fish.

Bear in mind to draw little bends, knocks and focuses to worry their mouths, noses and even the region were their tail starts.

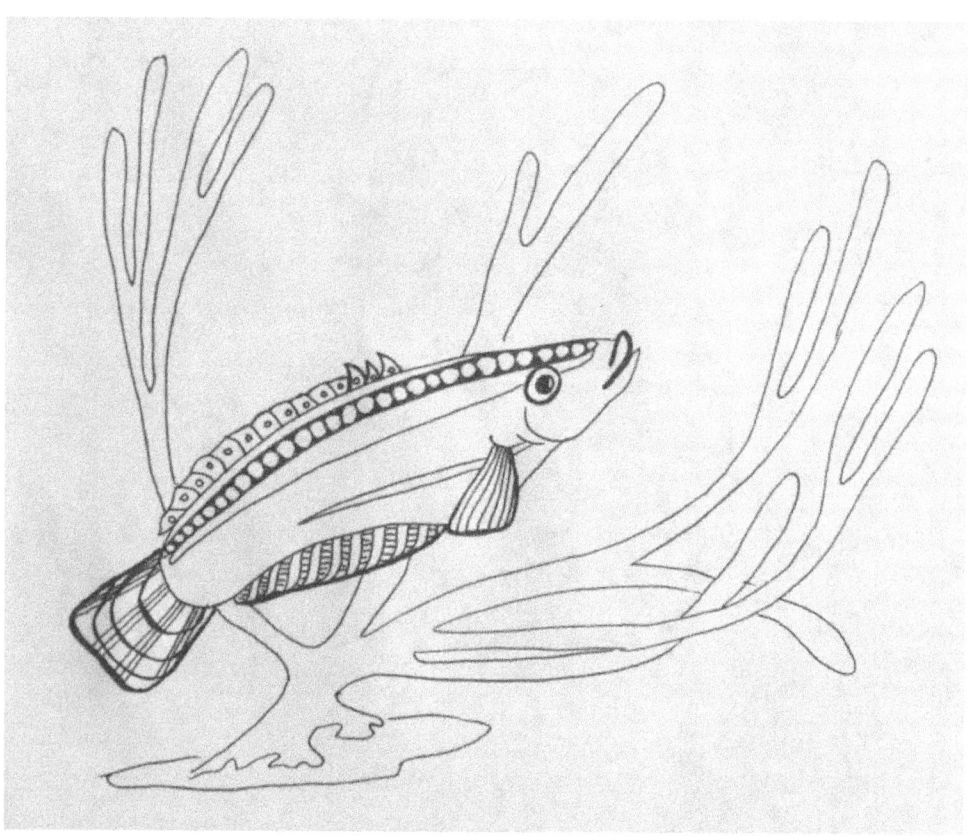

Step 2: Draw their tails. Make their tails on the right half of their body. Keep in mind that everyone is not the same as one another. Make the first tail by drawing wavy lines on its end, the second tail by drawing a little trapezoid shape, the third tail a round triangle and after that the fourth tail in a type of a "V" with wavy examples at its end.

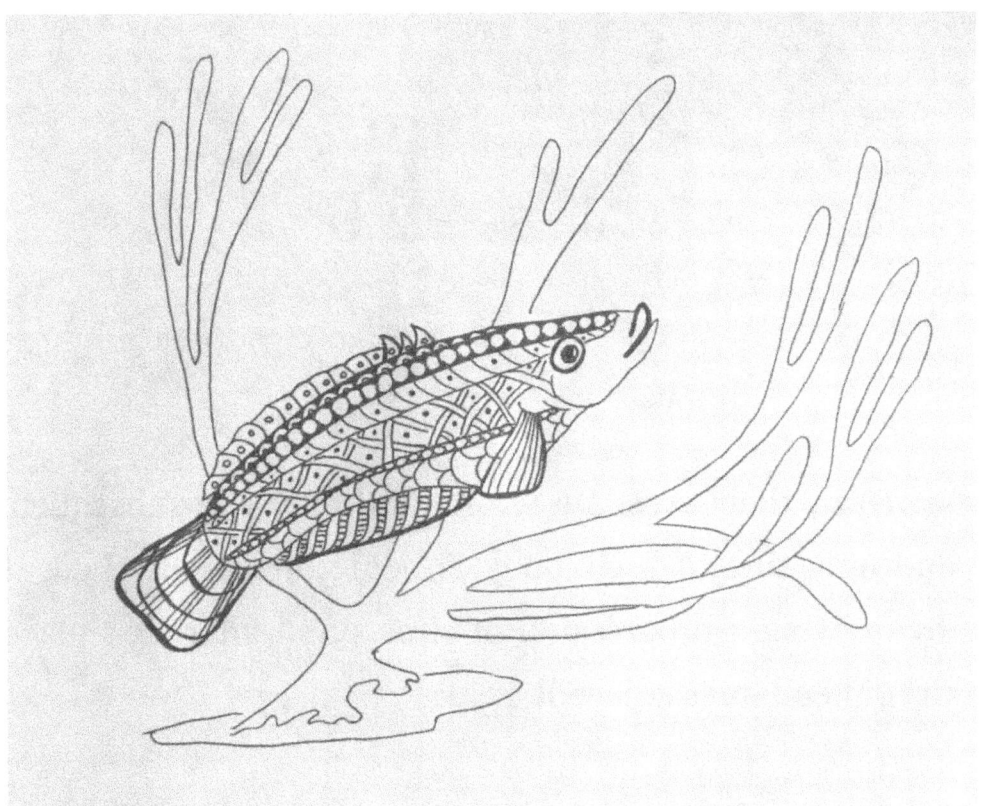

Step 3: Add their fins. Draw their balances by making influencing shapes, round shapes, crisscross shapes and wavy closures.

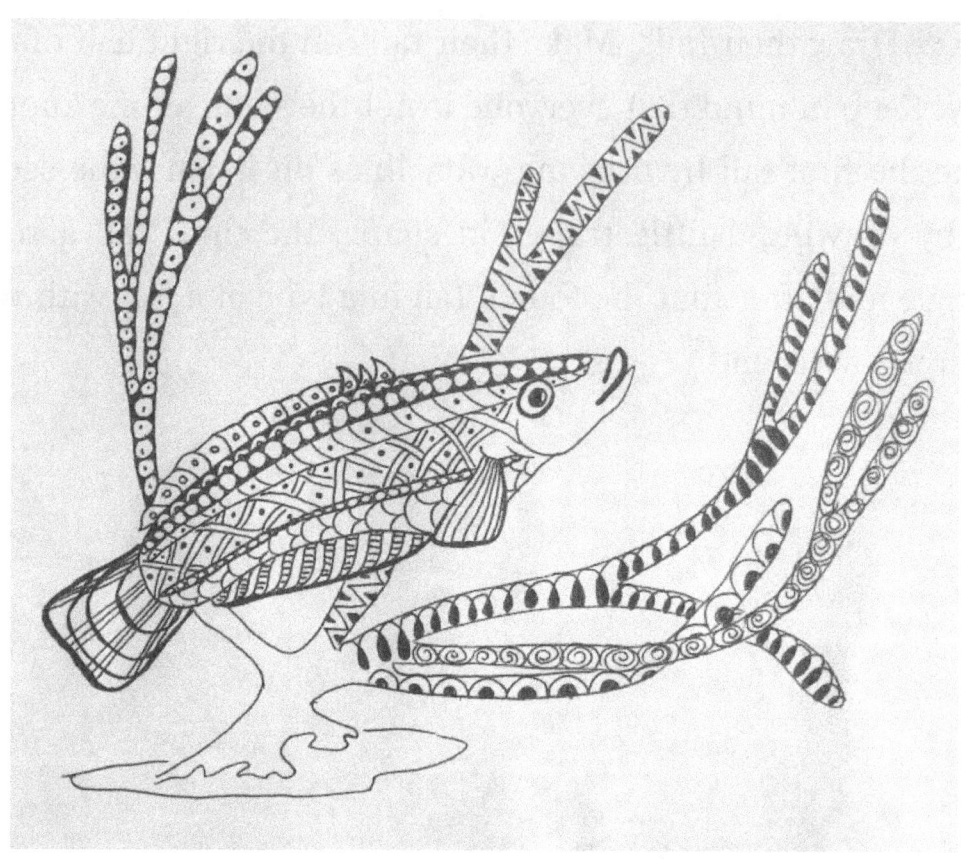

Step 4: Draw their eyes. Draw one and only eye subsequent to one and only side of their body is being appeared. Make their eyes by drawing a progression of circles and after that place an outskirt of bend lines adjacent to it.

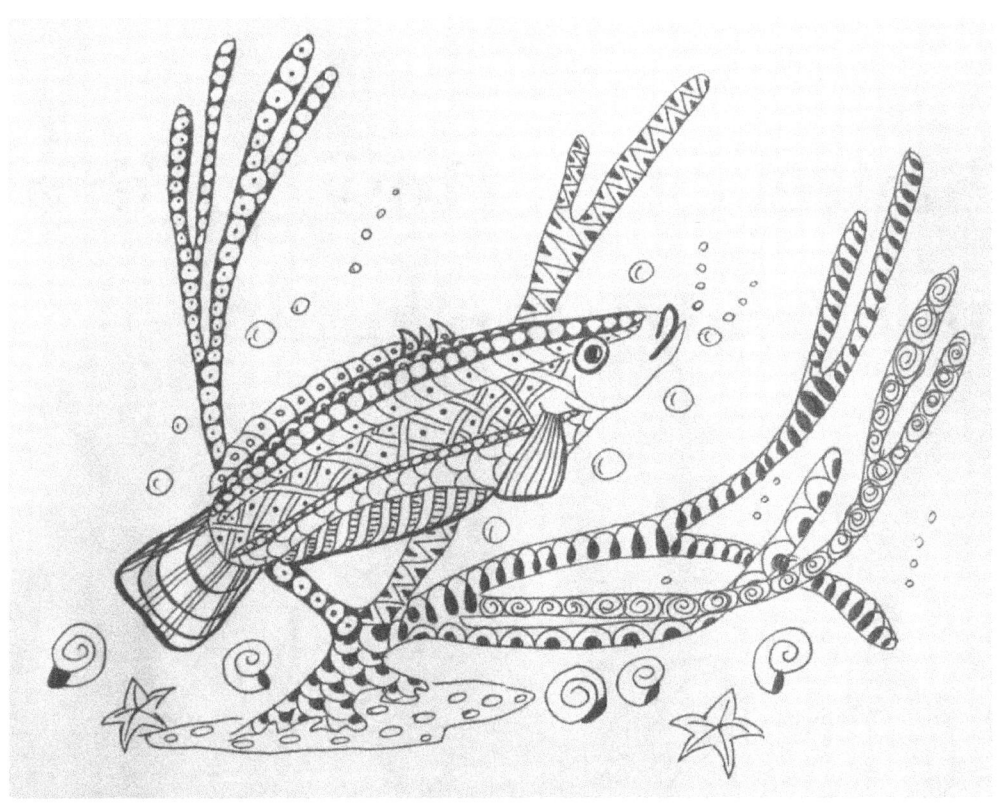

Step 5: Finish off your sketches by drawing the various types of examples on their body. Might it be thin or thick sickle shapes, circles or more wavy lines; the catch is to make everyone not quite the same as one another.

Chapter 3 – How to draw underwater mermaid

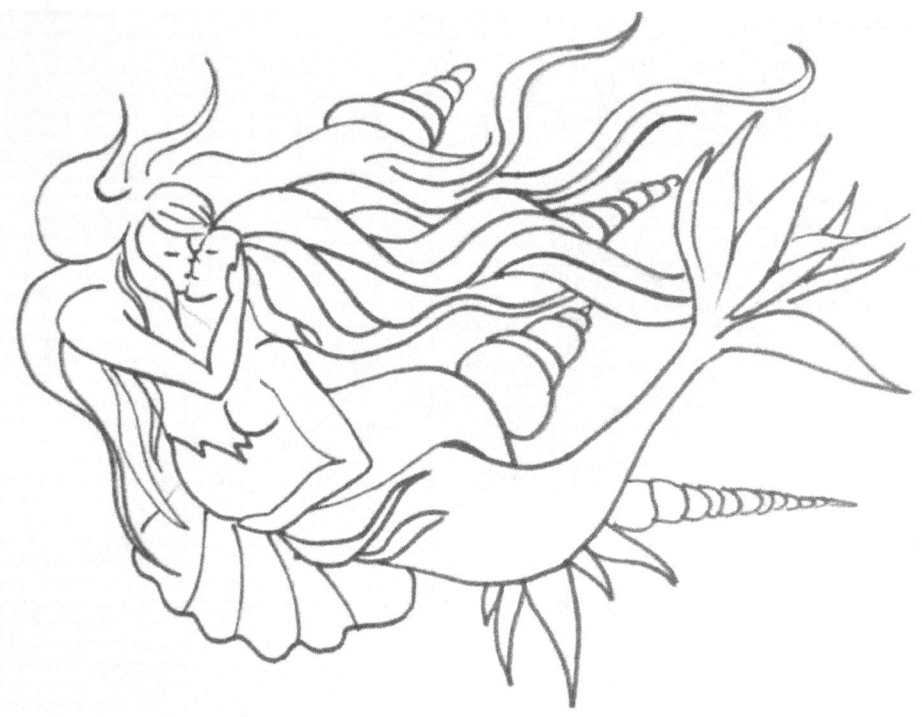

Step 1: Sketch the wireframe a human figure from head to waist, then draw a line to speak to the fishtail.

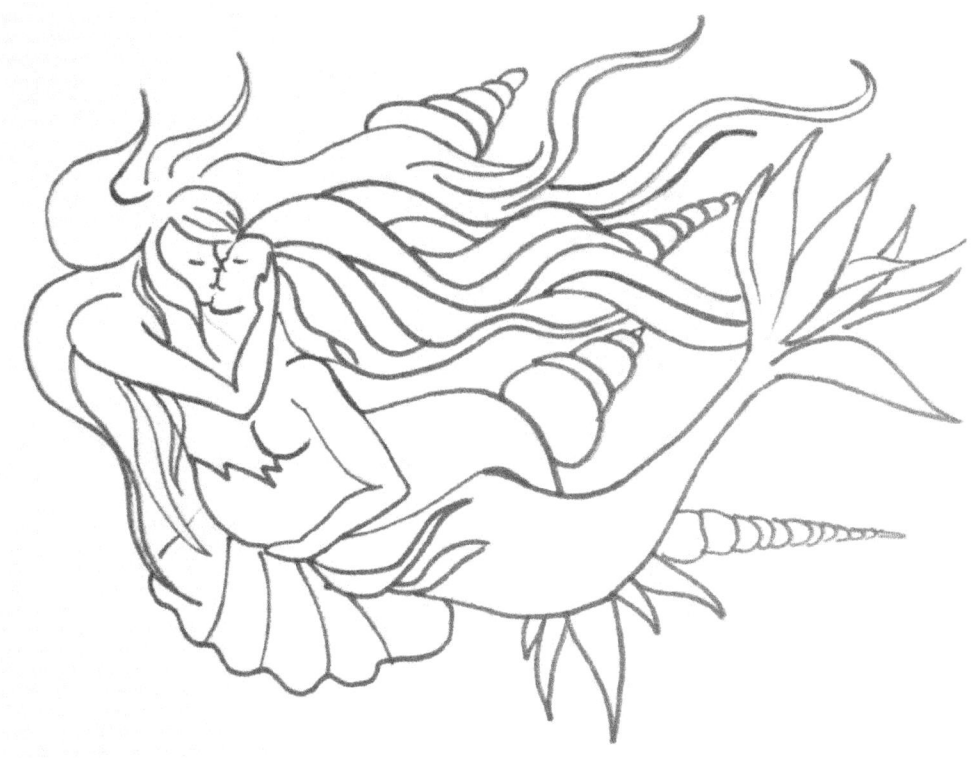

Step 2: Sketch extra shapes to manufacture the abdominal area then sketch the tail's state.

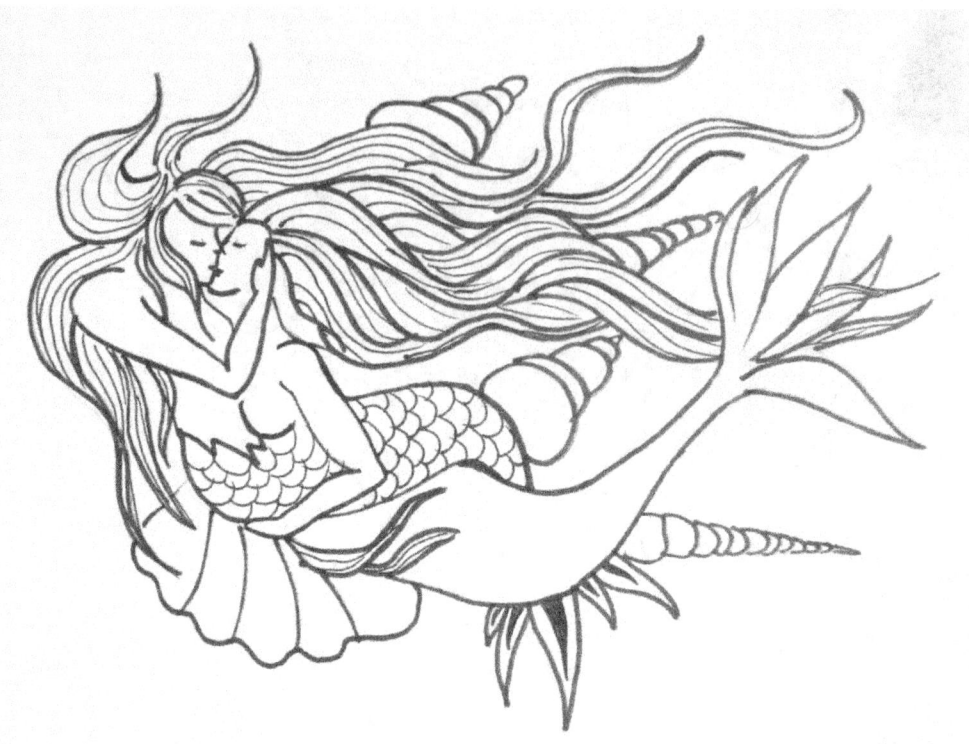

Step 3: Sketch the mermaid's figure.

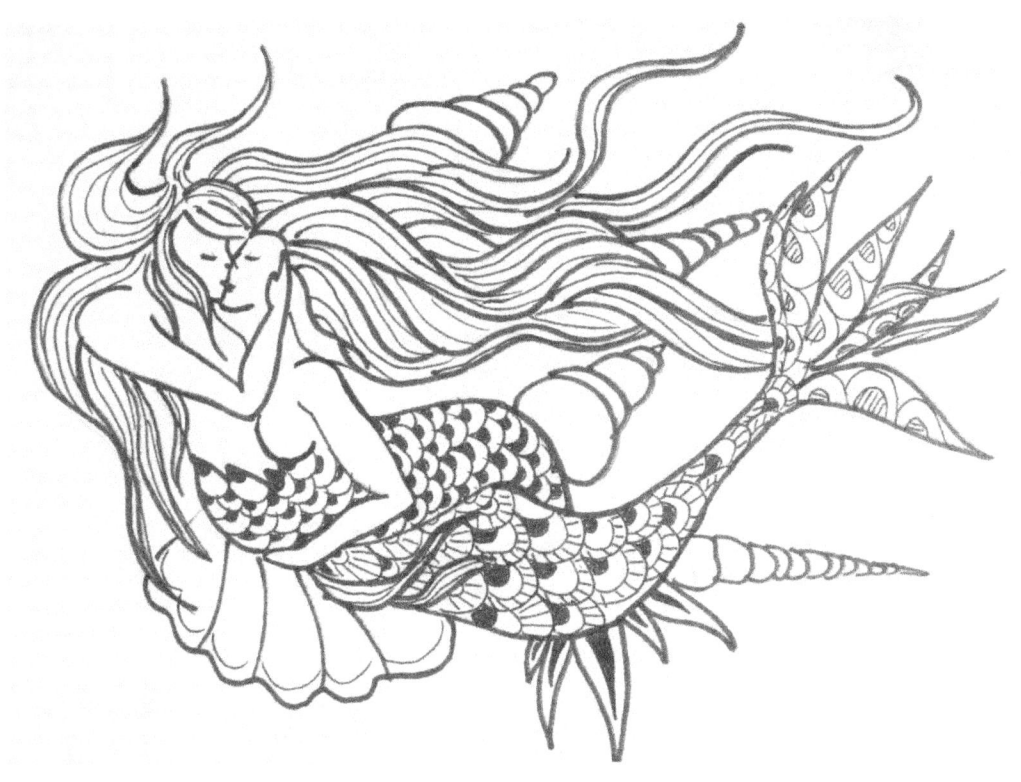

Step 4: Add the hair, balances, and different points of interest.

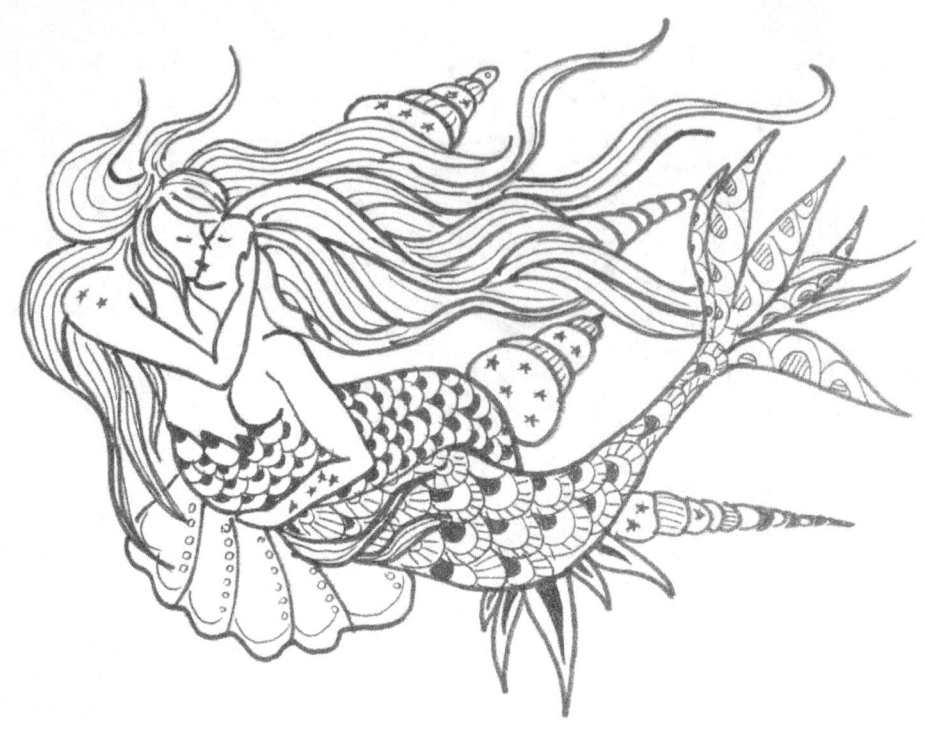

Step 5: Add skin examples or embellishing elements if necessary.

Step 6: Refine the craftsmanship utilizing a littler tipped drawing instrument.

Chapter 4 – How to draw a Crab

It is safe to say that you are an immense aficionado of ocean animals? Do you adore crabs? Crabs are fun, intriguing, and easy to draw. Both experienced and new specialists can appreciate drawing crabs with this simple orderly instructional exercise. Draw crabs for adornments at a pool party or only for the sake of entertainment. Take after the progressions underneath to figure out how.

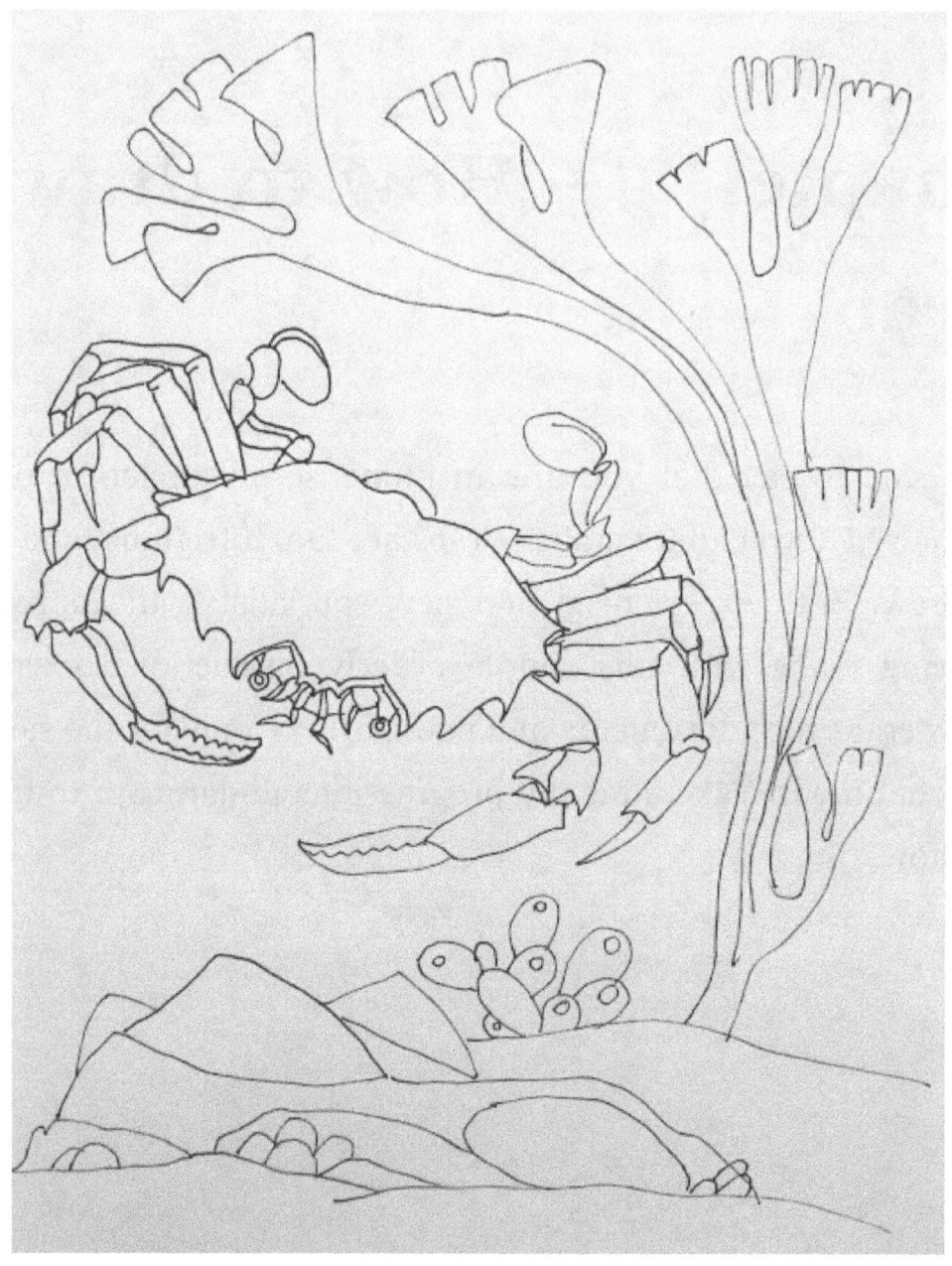

Step 1: Set up your workstation. Locate an agreeable sufficiently bright work environment where every one of your materials are close-by. For this instructional exercise, you will require:

- Your sketchbook, paper, or card stock

- A pencil

- An eraser

- Scissors (discretionary)

- Markers, color pencils, or pastels (discretionary)

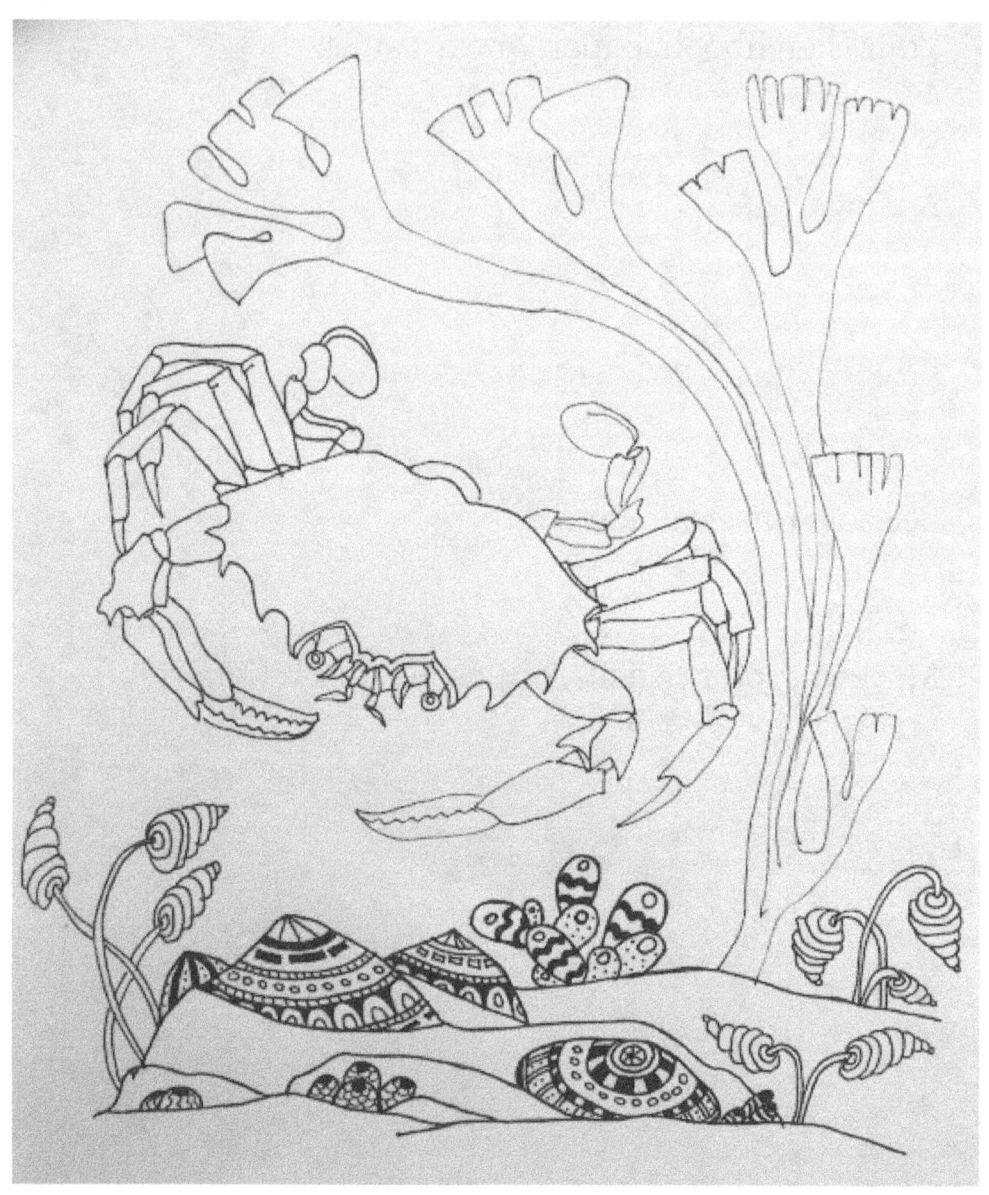

Step 2: Draw medium measured oval, long-routes in the focal point of your paper. Make a point to give yourself a lot of room on the top, base, and sides of your oval. This will be the crab's body.

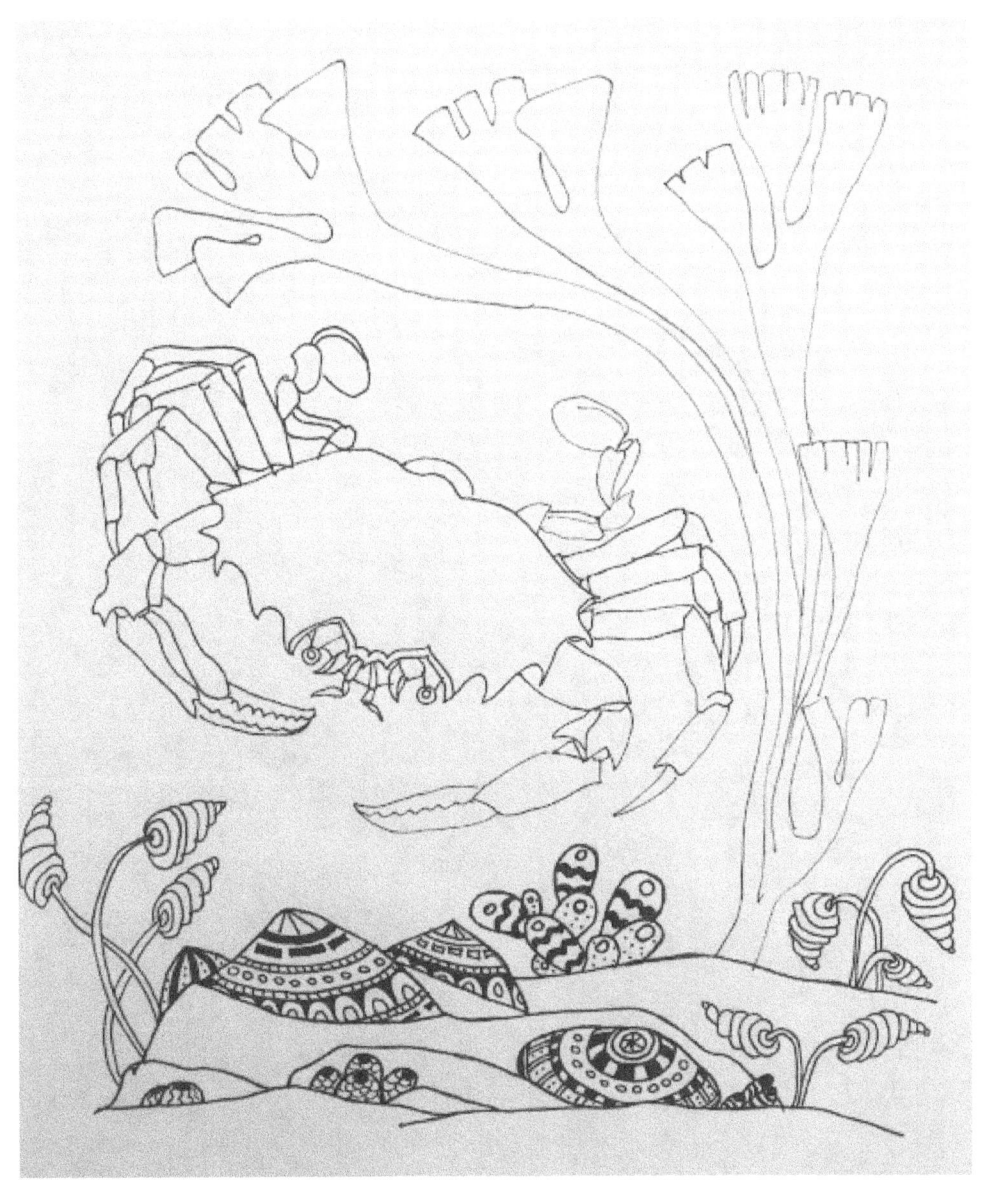

Step 3: Create the crab's state. Crab shells are harsh and pointy around the greater part of their edges. Take your pencil and add edge point of interest to the crab's shell.

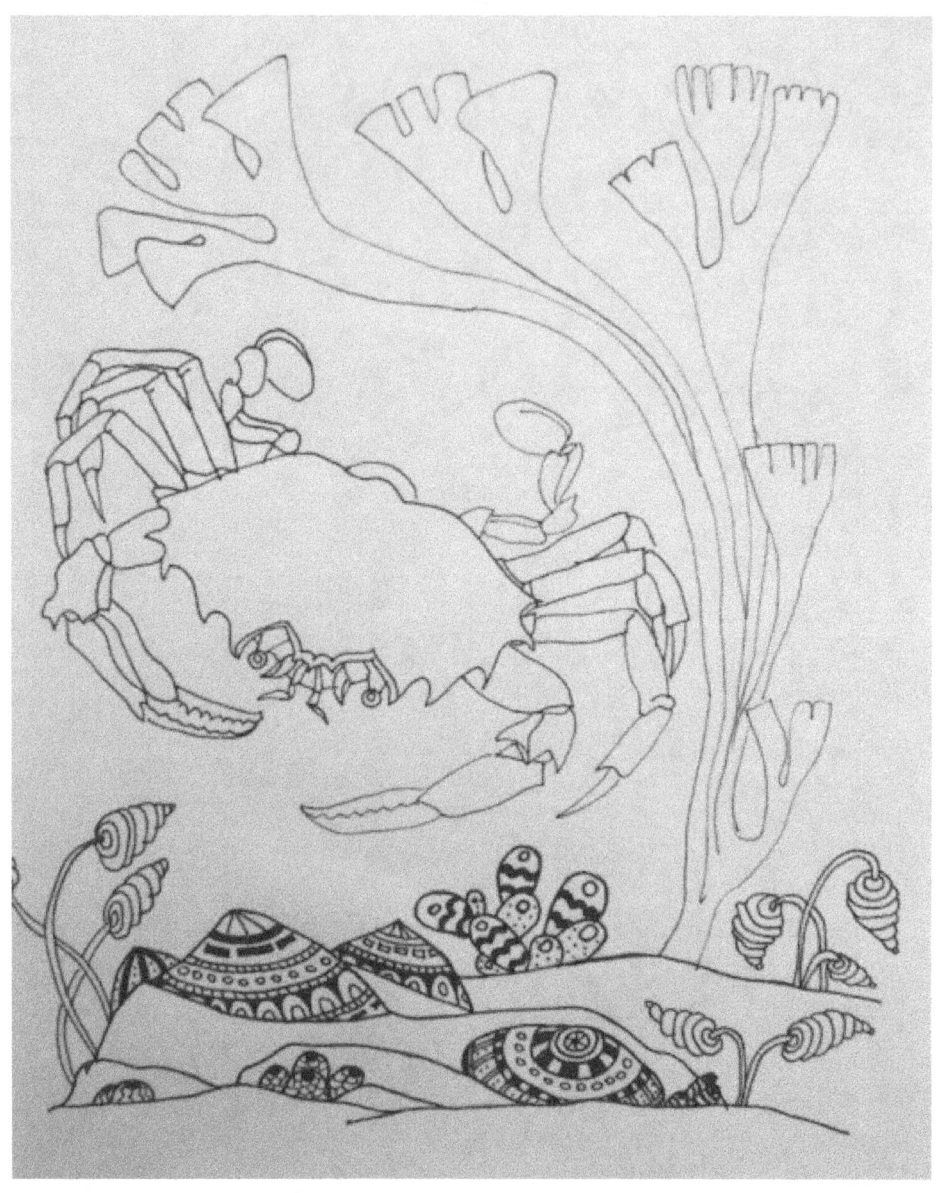

Step 4: You can draw this oval in one constant stroke or interface two sideways "C" shapes to make this shape.

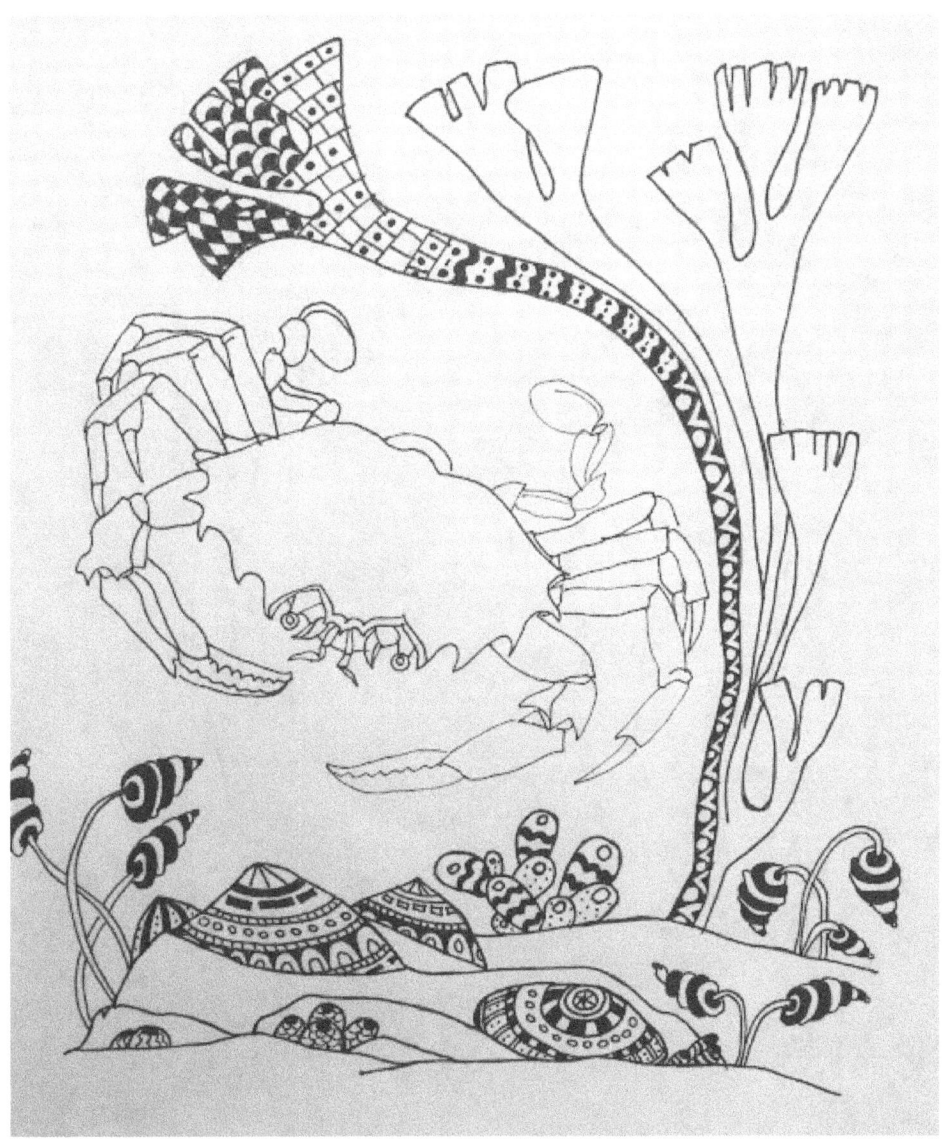

Step 5: Add the eyes and receiving wire. Crabs have two little eyes with a small receiving wire originating from every one, similar to eyebrows. You will need to draw these at the highest point of your oval in the center.

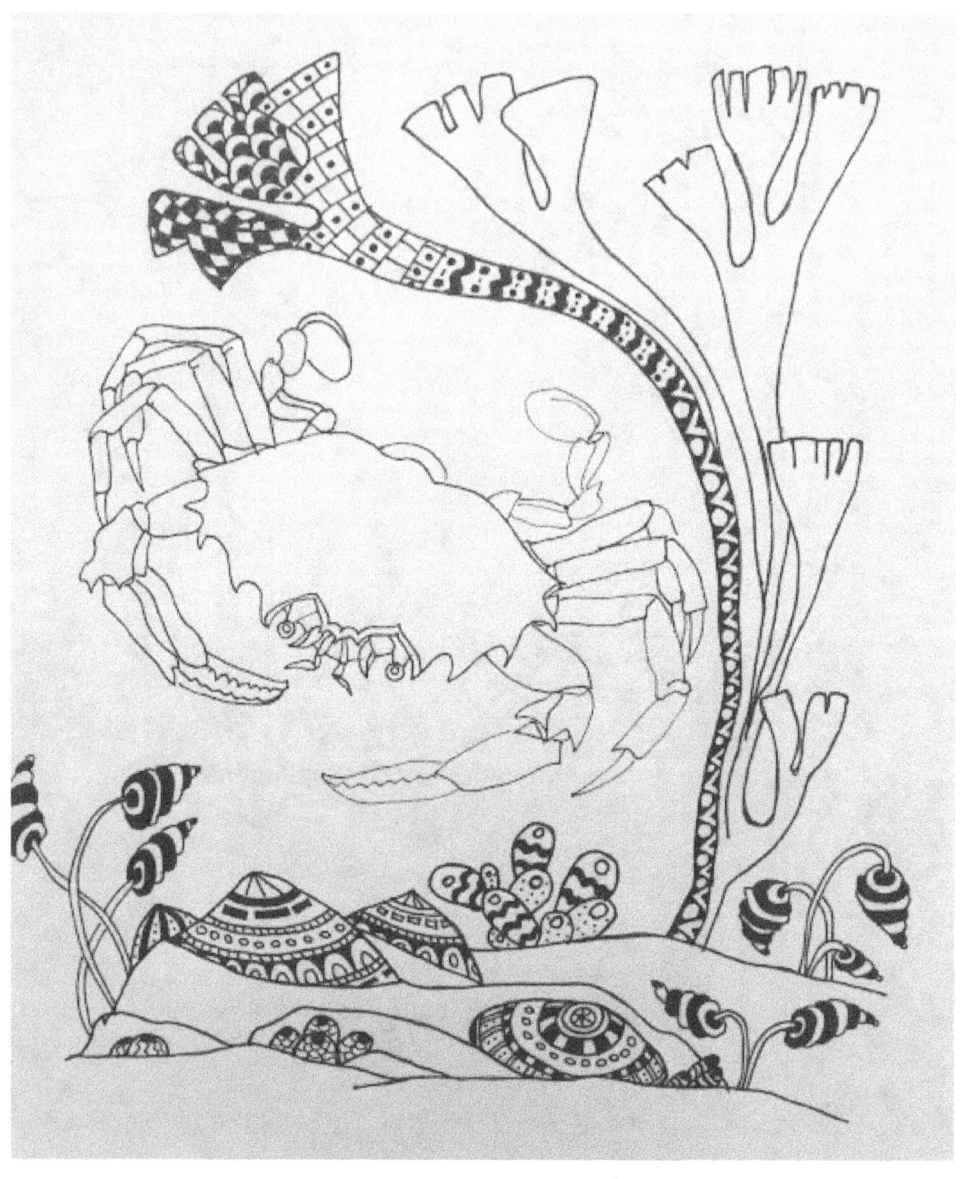

Locate the focal point of your oval and draw two little circles beside one another on the top line. Make a point to space the circles sufficiently far away that you can obviously see them two. You might likewise need to color them in totally with your pencil or a dark marker.

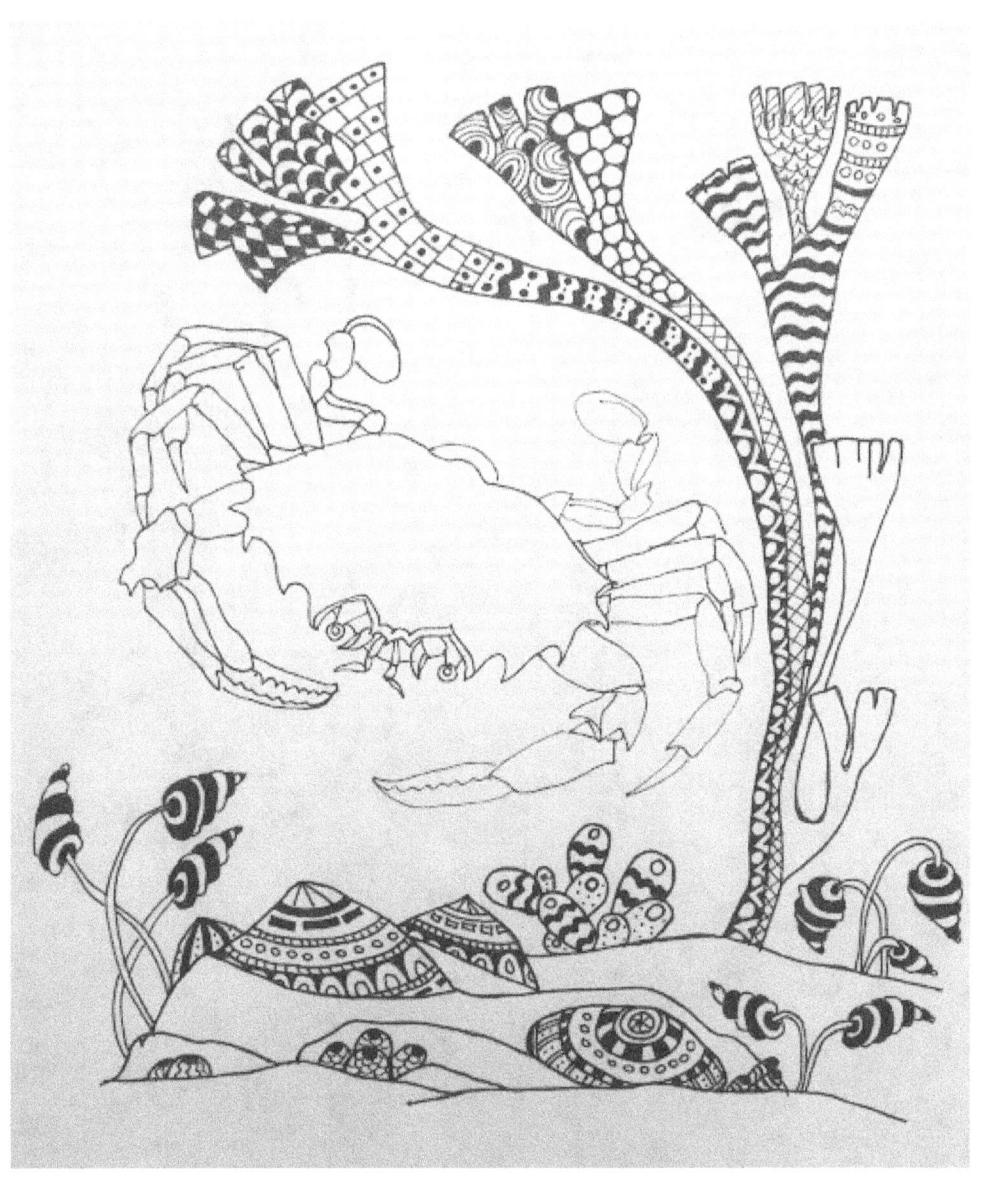

Over every circle, include a short line staying up and out, from within the circle. This implies that the two radio wire lines ought to be specifically opposite one another, with the circle eyes all things considered.

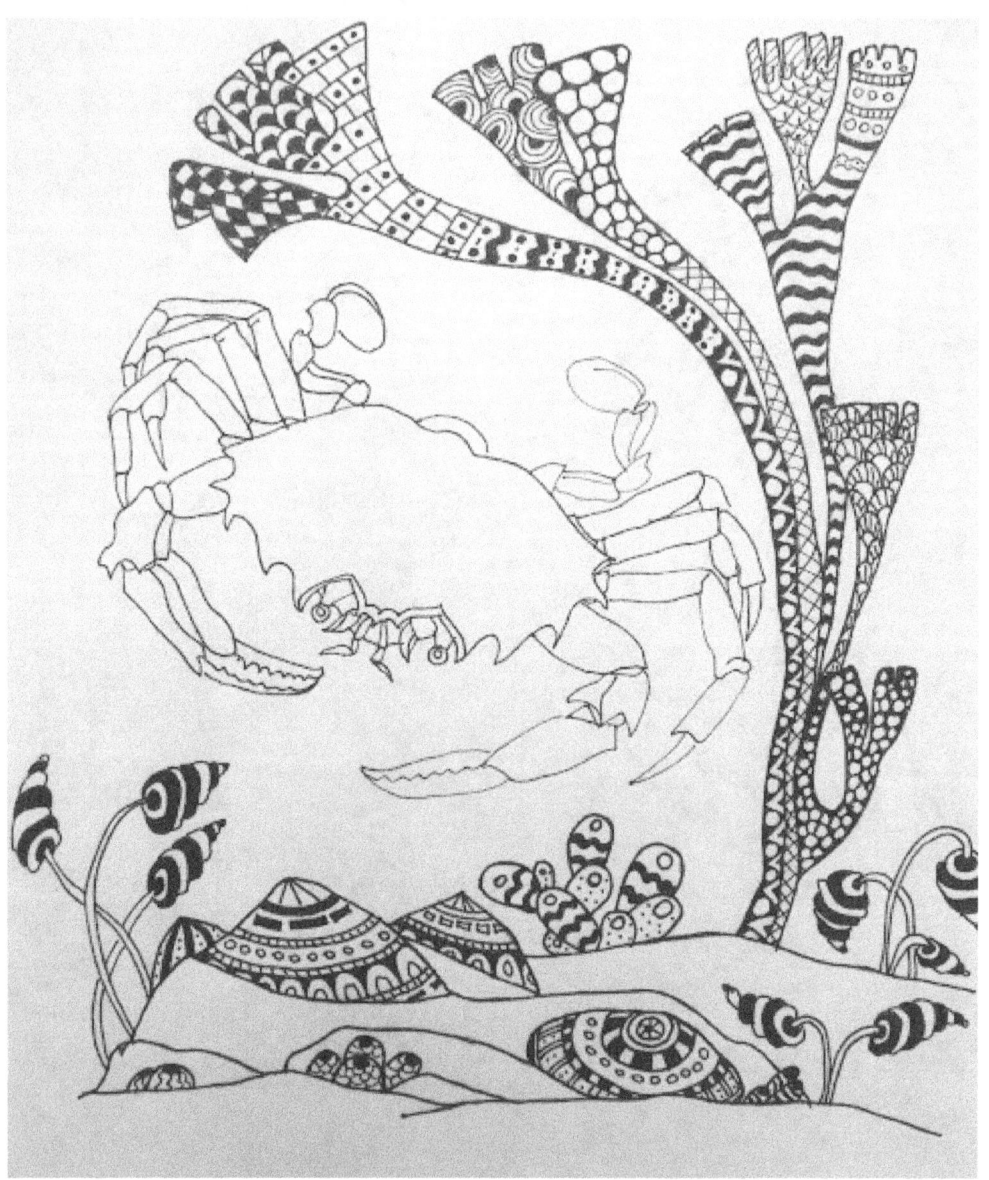

Step 6: Draw the claws. Drawing the claws of your crab is a three stage process. On the highest point of the oval, around the edges, include little oval, tall-courses, to every side. In the event that you experience difficulty getting these ovals the same size, don't stress, a few crabs have one hook that is bigger than the other.

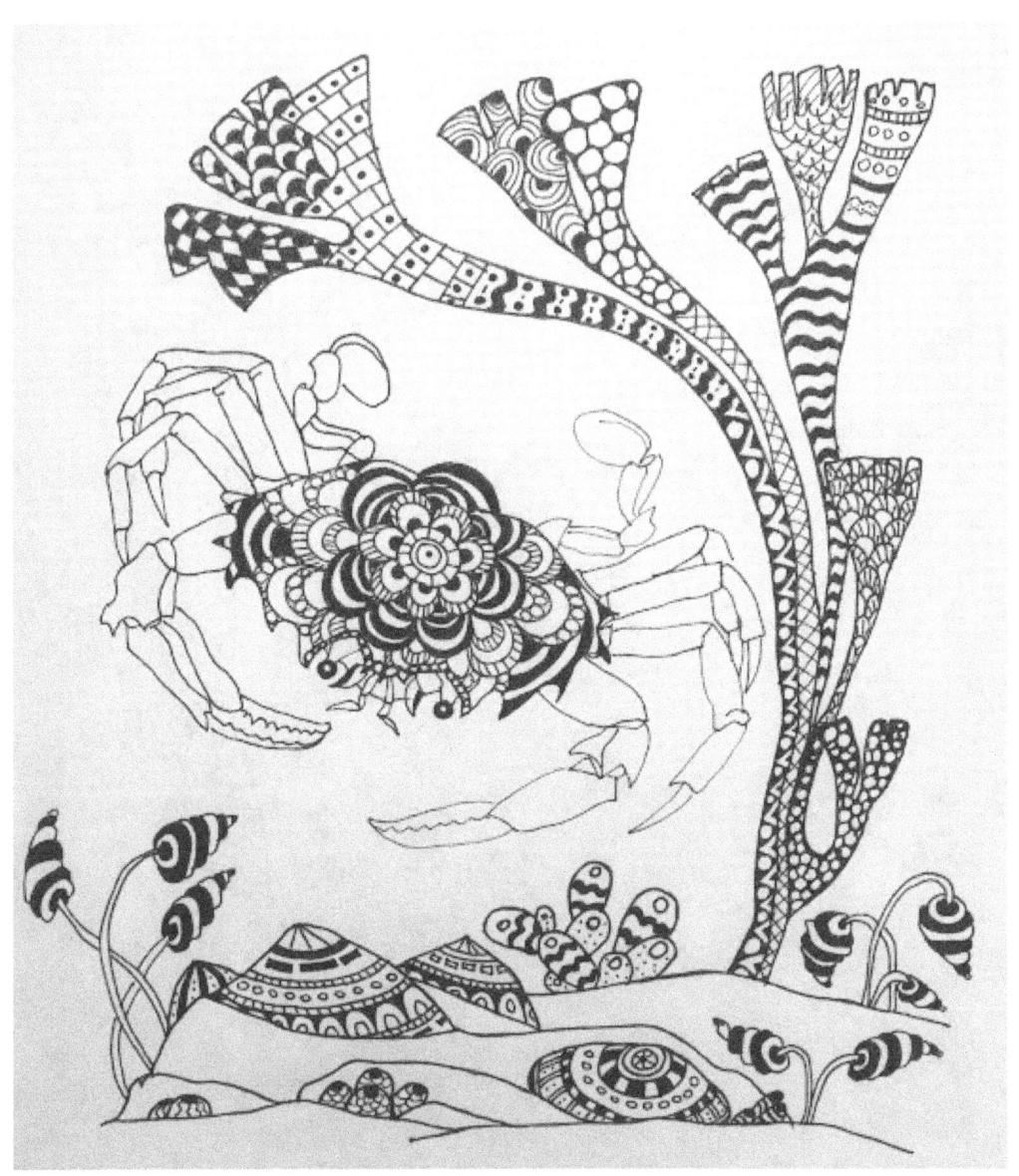

On top of every oval, draw a bigger oval tilted askew internal toward the eyes. Your top ovals ought to seem as though they are verging on confronting one another while coming to upward.

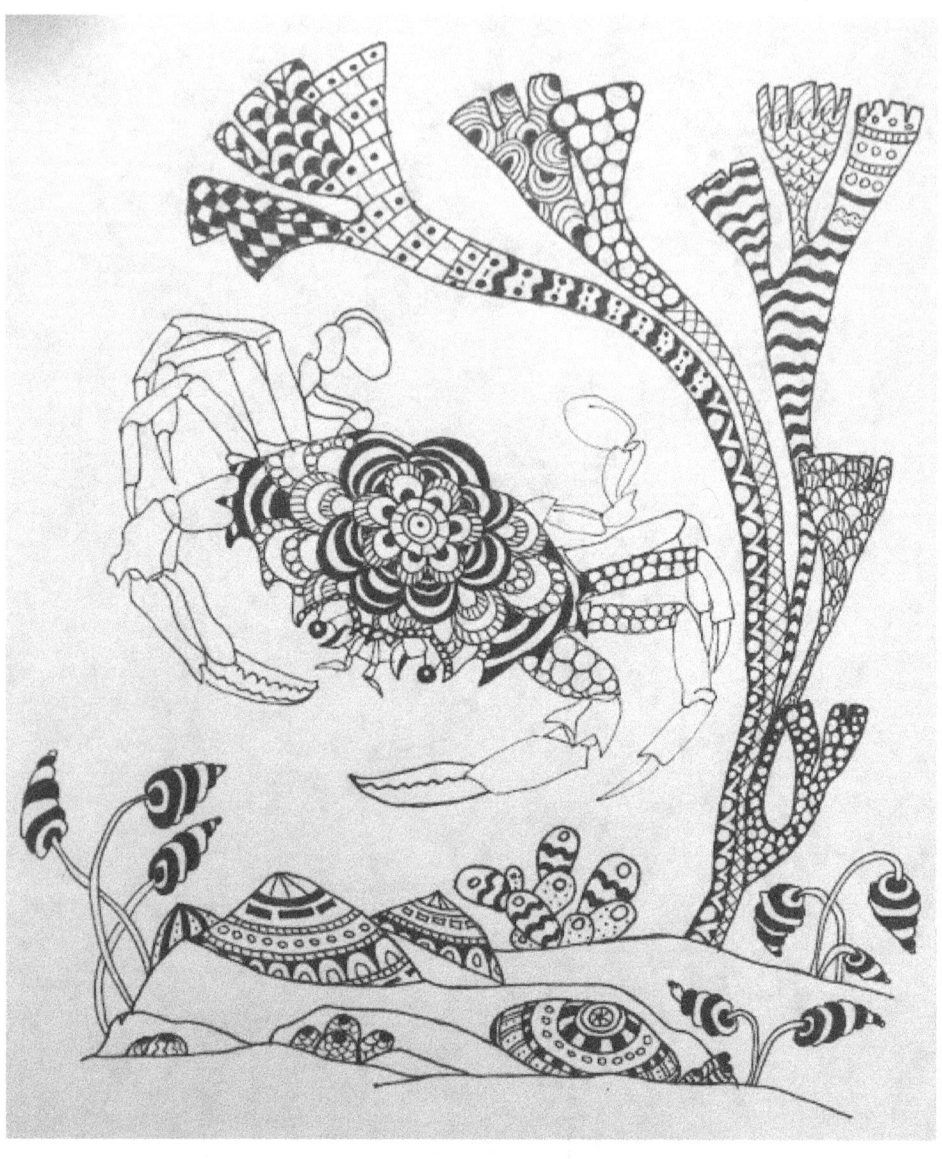

Include the pliers the highest point of the bigger oval. To draw
the pliers, hold your pencil at the highest point of the oval and
draw a short bended line coming to upward. End this line with a
pointed tip, and bring the line down to the focal point of the
highest point of the oval.

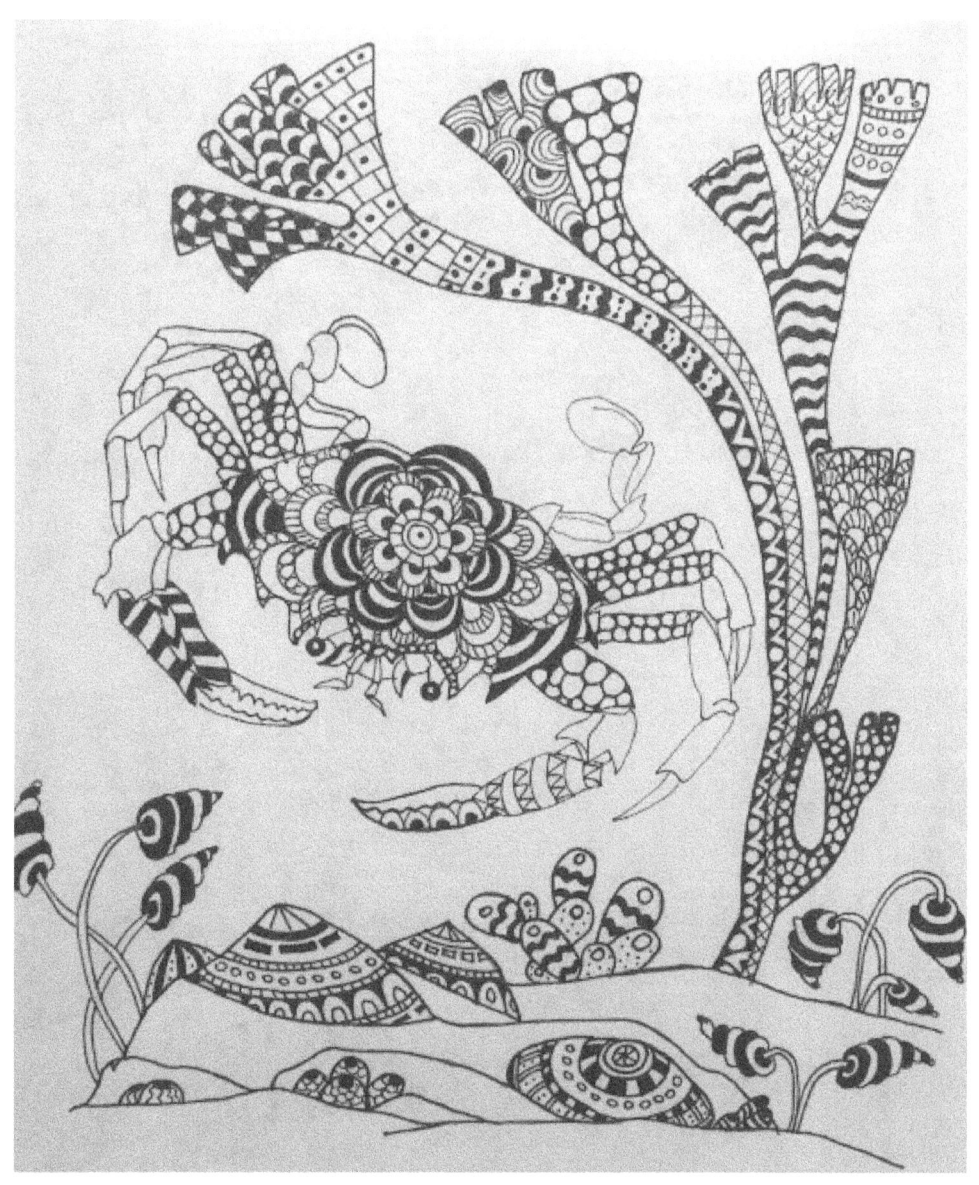

From the focal point of the highest point of the oval, draw a shorter bended line, bending toward the first (as though to finish a circle), and end that line in a point too, before bringing it withdraw the oval's base.

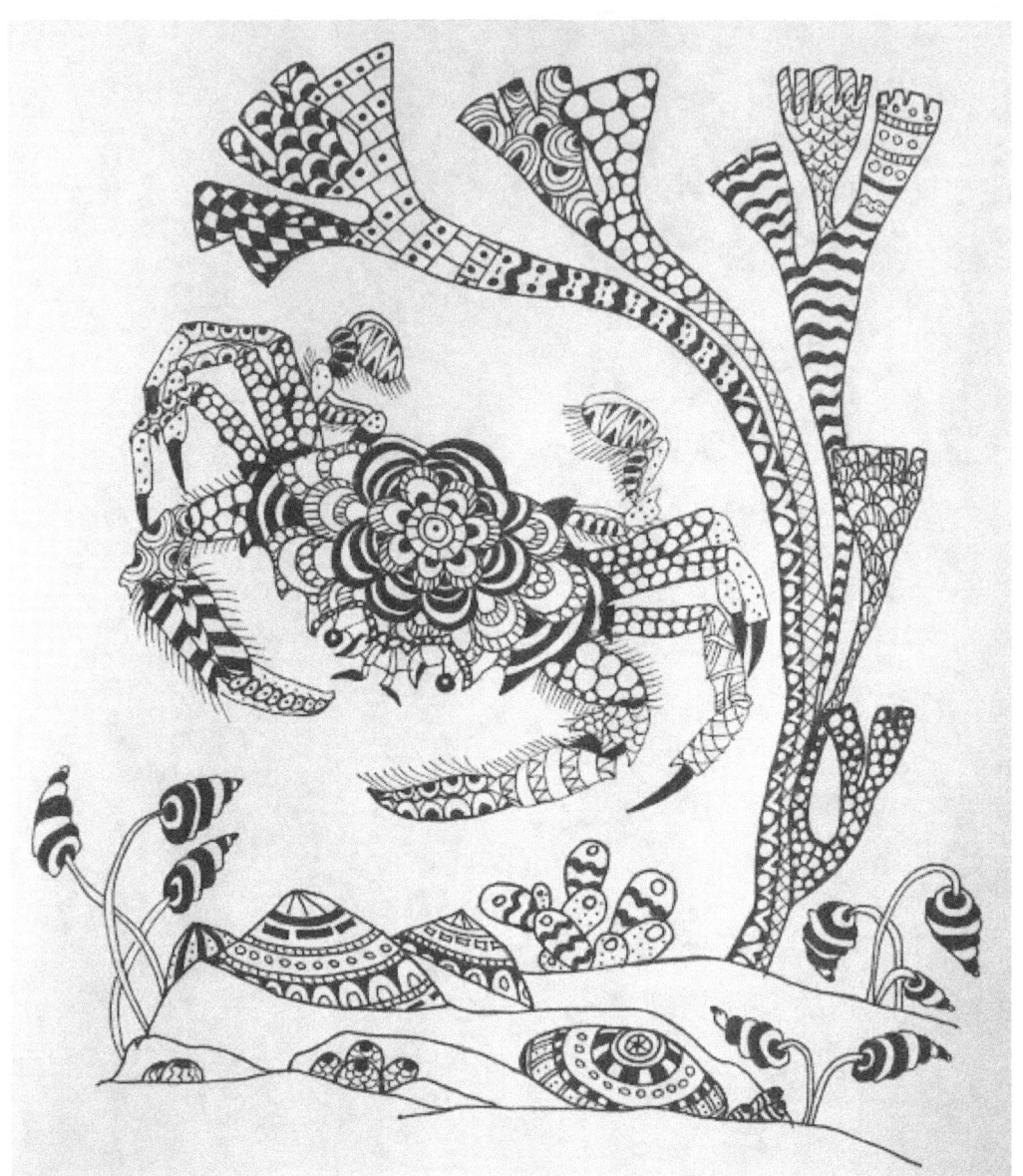

Step 7: Draw the legs. Your crab can have three legs on every side, all underneath the claws. Begin the first leg specifically beneath the hook. Draw a bow shape guiding upward, in accordance with the paw's heading. Rehash this on the other side.

Draw another leg specifically underneath the first. Utilize a present shape to point this leg upward also. Rehash on the other side.

Draw the last leg specifically underneath the second, however this time, point the present shape descending. Rehash on the other side.

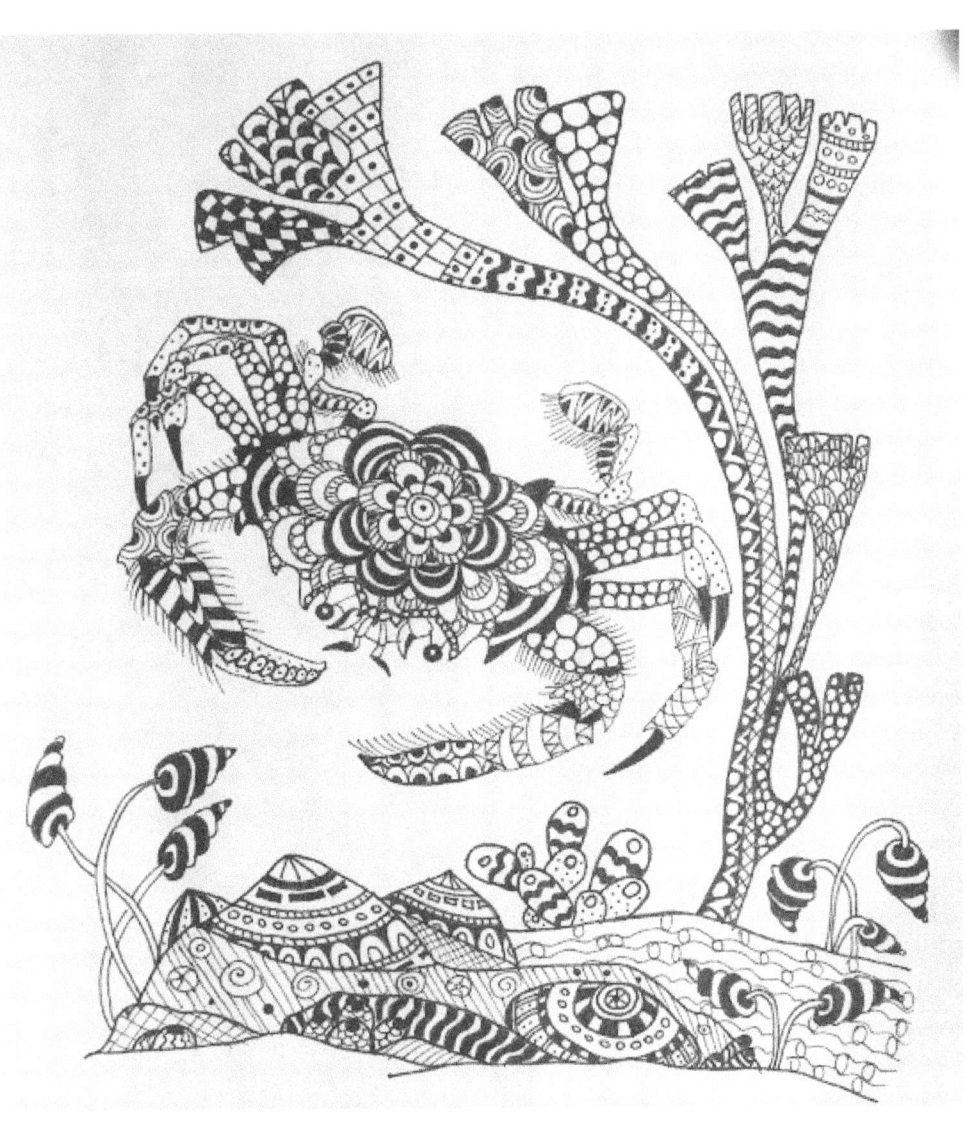

Step 8: Finish your crab. Contingent upon what you need to do, there are a couple of ways you can complete your crab. You may wish to color your crab and after that cut it out, utilizing it as a gathering adornment for an underwater topic. You could likewise add an underwater scene to your paper, drawing a kelp woodland or ocean otters around your crab. Have some good times!

Chapter 5 – How to draw an Octopus

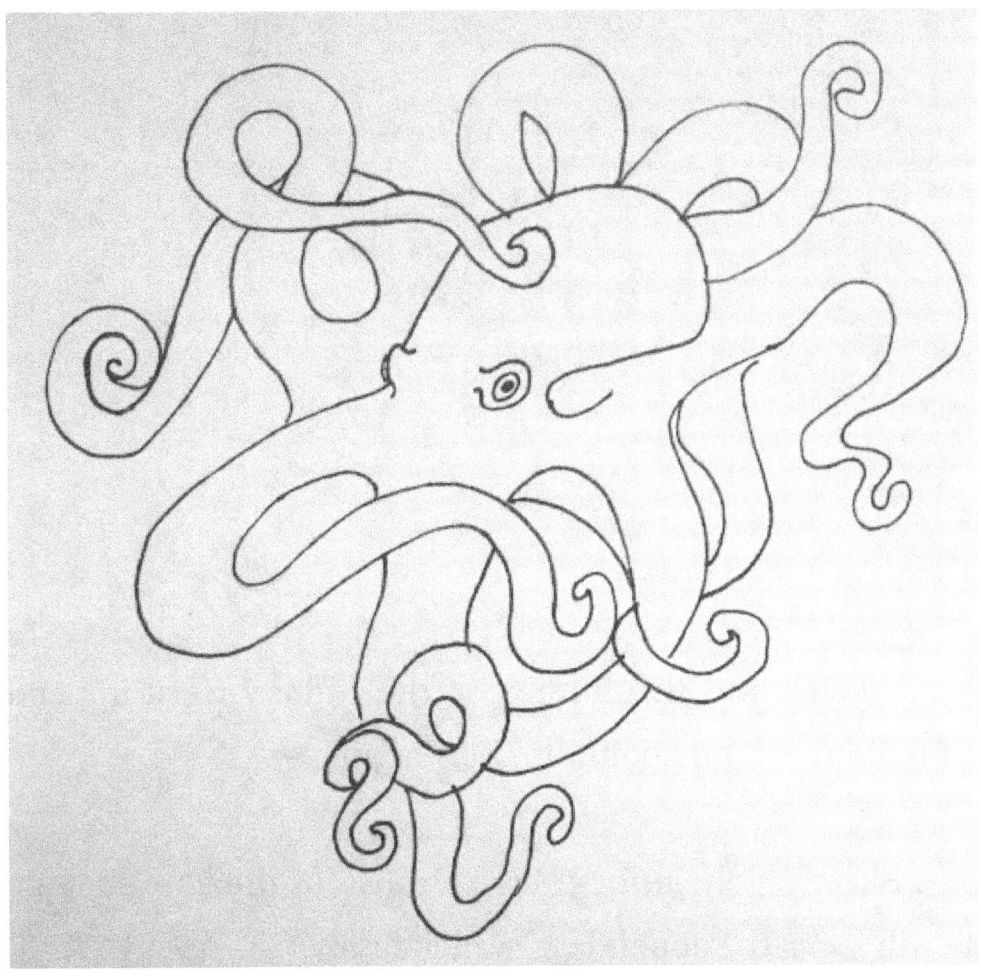

Step 1: Sketch the essential states of the octopus.

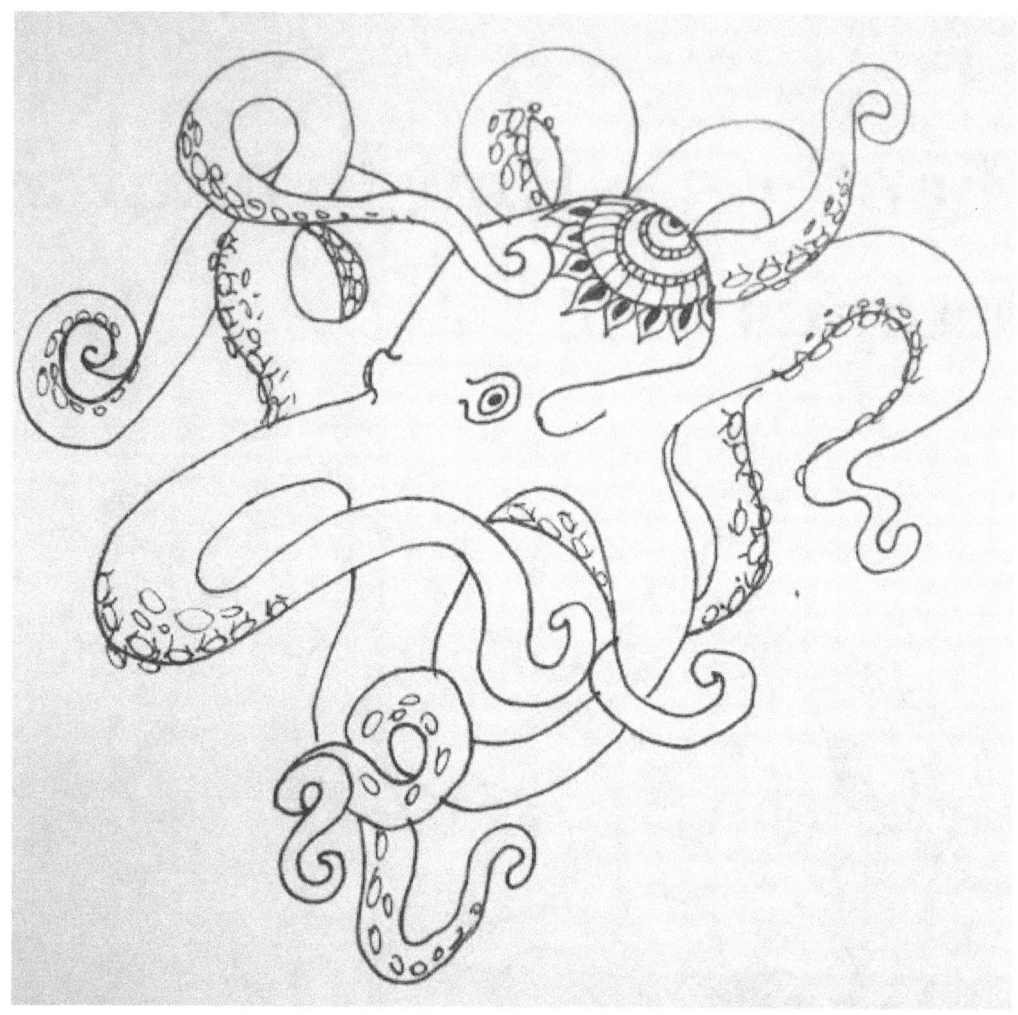

Step 2: Sketch the wireframe for the limbs. every appendage ought to join with one point on the star shape.

Step 3: Sketch a circle for every purpose of the star shape. The circle will focus the appendage's thickness.

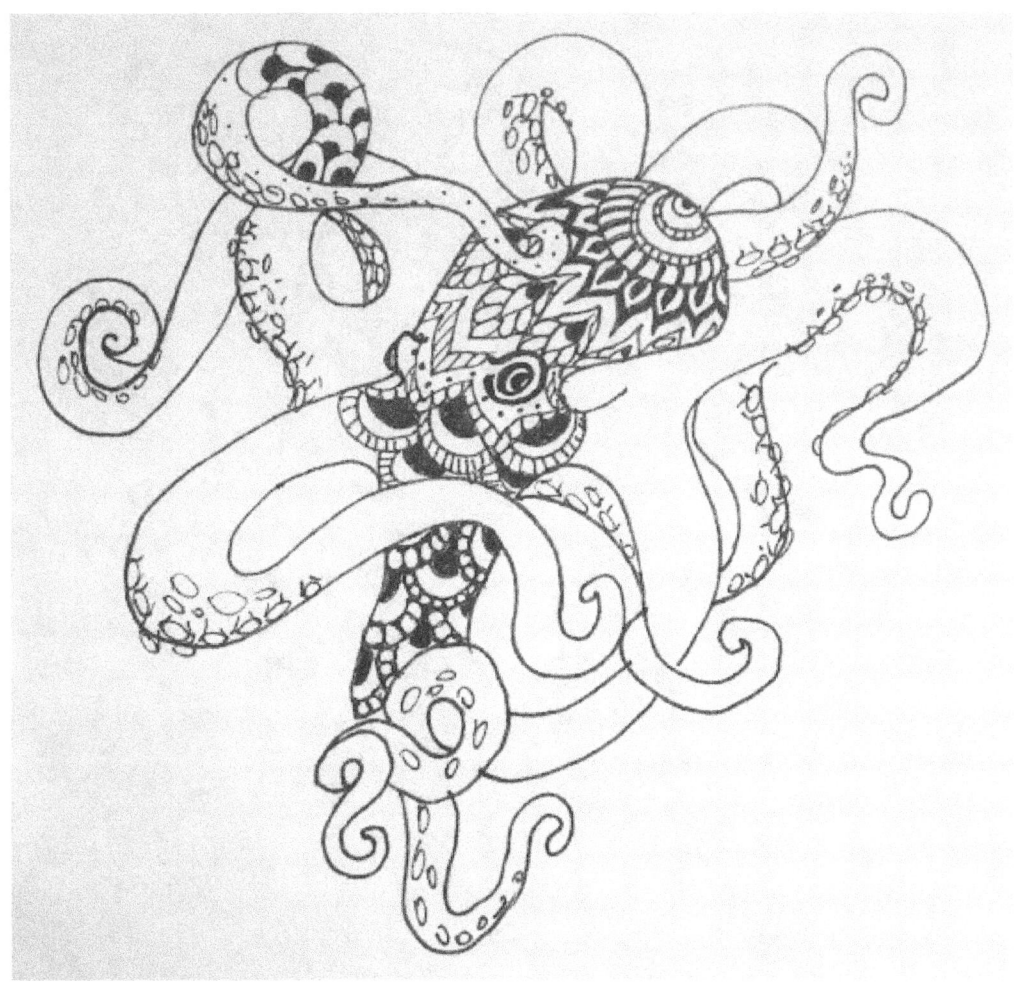

Step 4: Sketch the shapes for the appendages utilizing octopus pictures as references.

Step 5: Sketch extra points of interest for the suckers and the eyes.

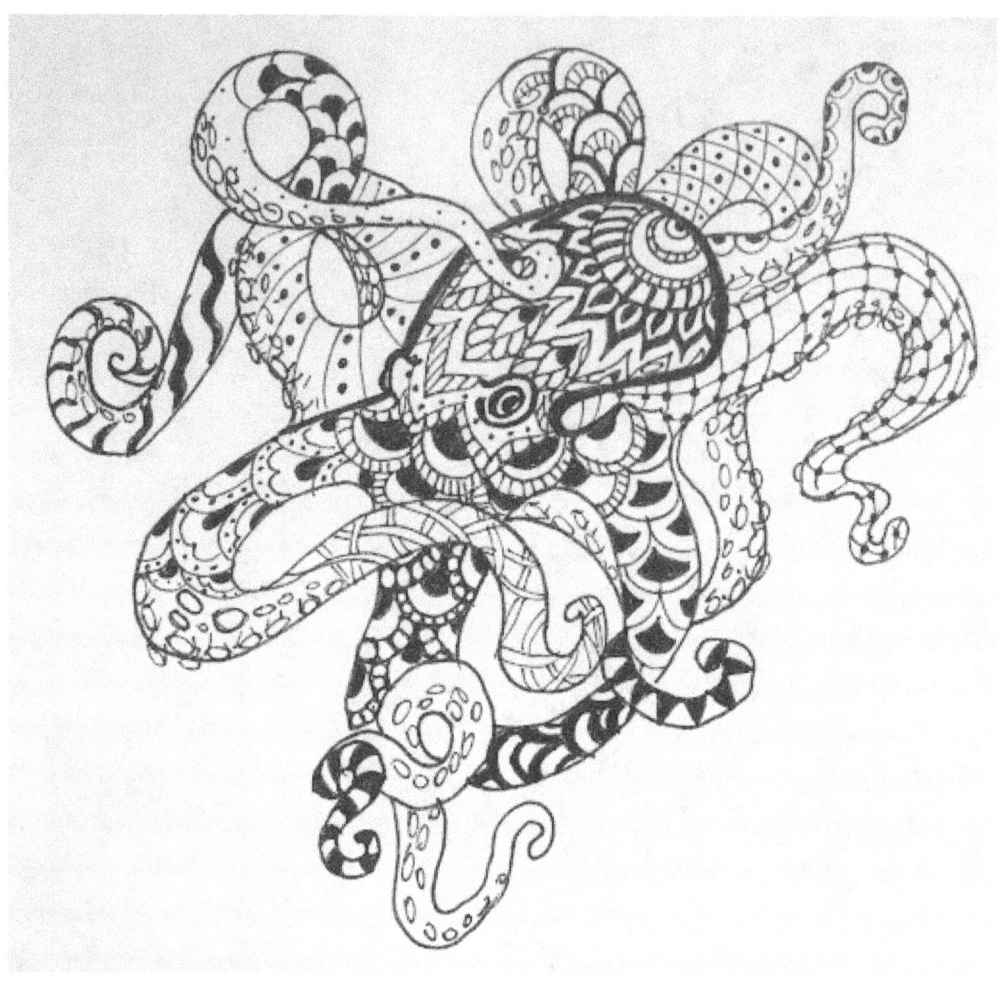

Step 6: Refine the sketch utilizing a littler tipped drawing apparatus.

Step 7: Erase and uproot the sketch marks.

Chapter 6 – How to draw many fishes

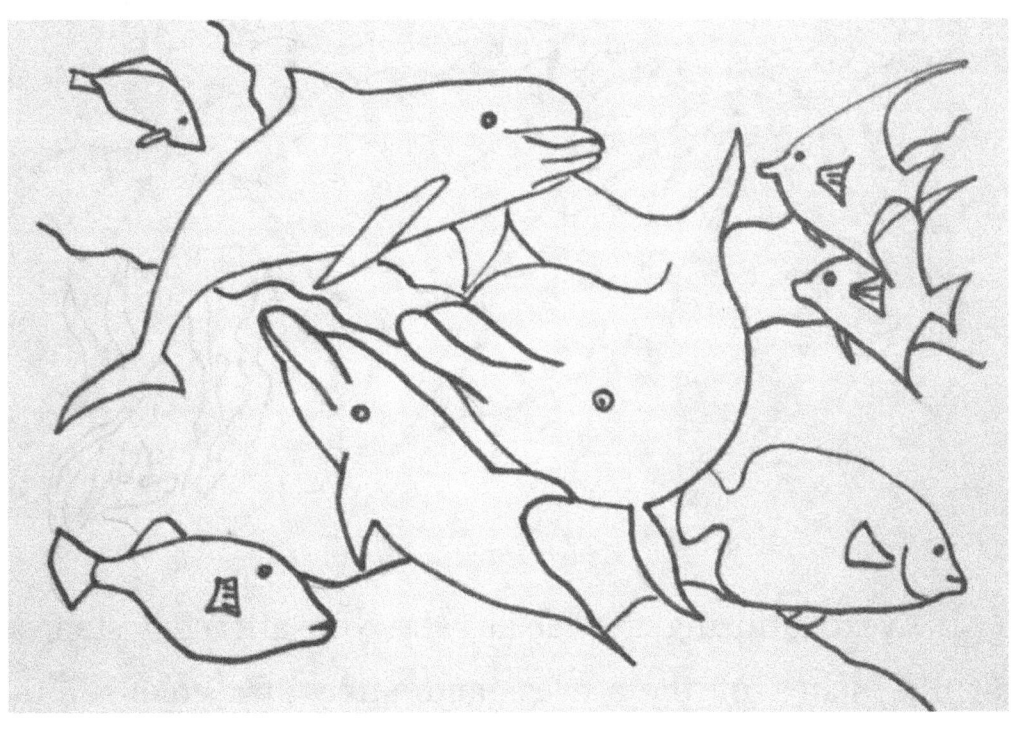

Step 1: We should draw some fish might we? Begin with three circle shapes. Make certain to draw the circles in distinctive sizes to add mixture to the fish. Next draw in the facial rules as you see here. You will ultimately draw a basic diagram of their bodies as you see here.

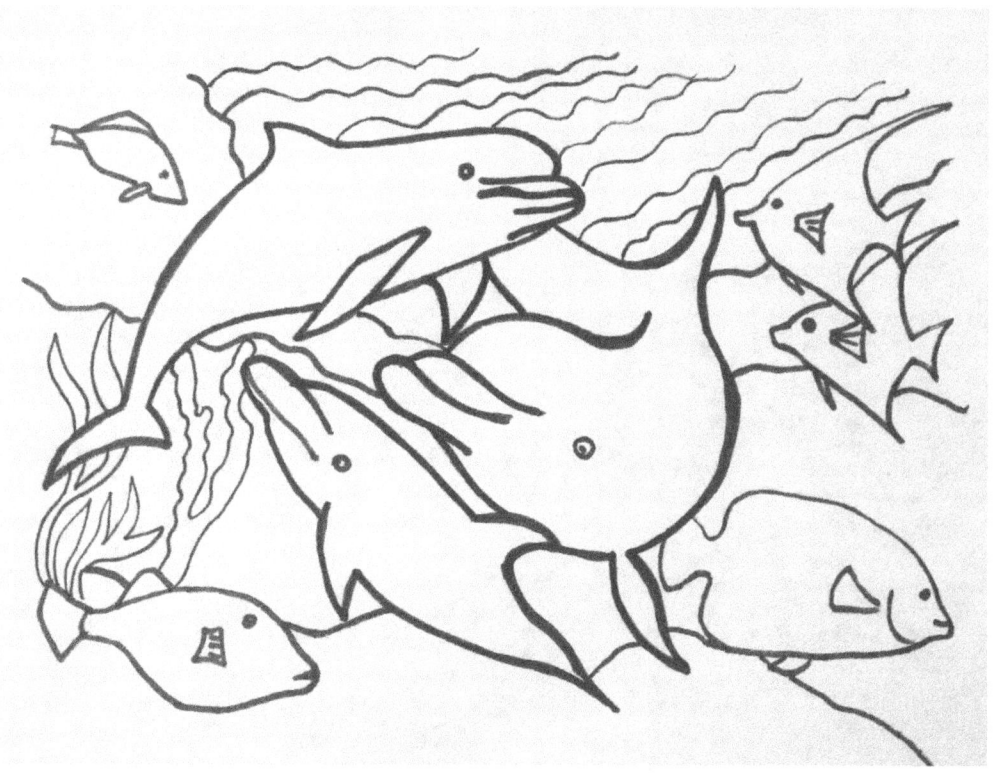

Step 2: Next, utilizing the facial rules you attracted step one, draw the states of their eyes, and after that color in their students. You will then draw their fish lips and add some definition to these fish countenances like eyebrows, and space around their appearances as you see here. The bigger fish gets his first blade drawn in before you go too.

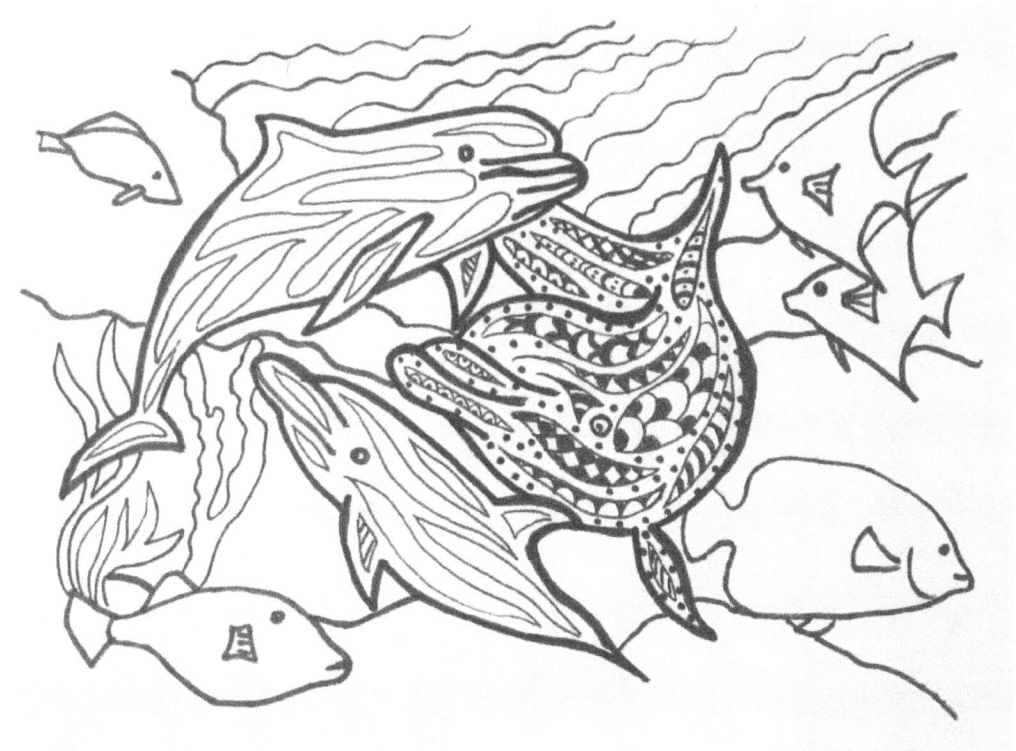

Step 3: You are as of now verging on finished with this instructional exercise "how to draw fish". You will begin step three by sketching out their dorsal balances (which is the blades on the highest points of their bodies) and the caudal balances on the two fish above. The caudal balance is otherwise called the tail balance coincidentally. For the expansive fish, simply draw the starting line of his tail balance.

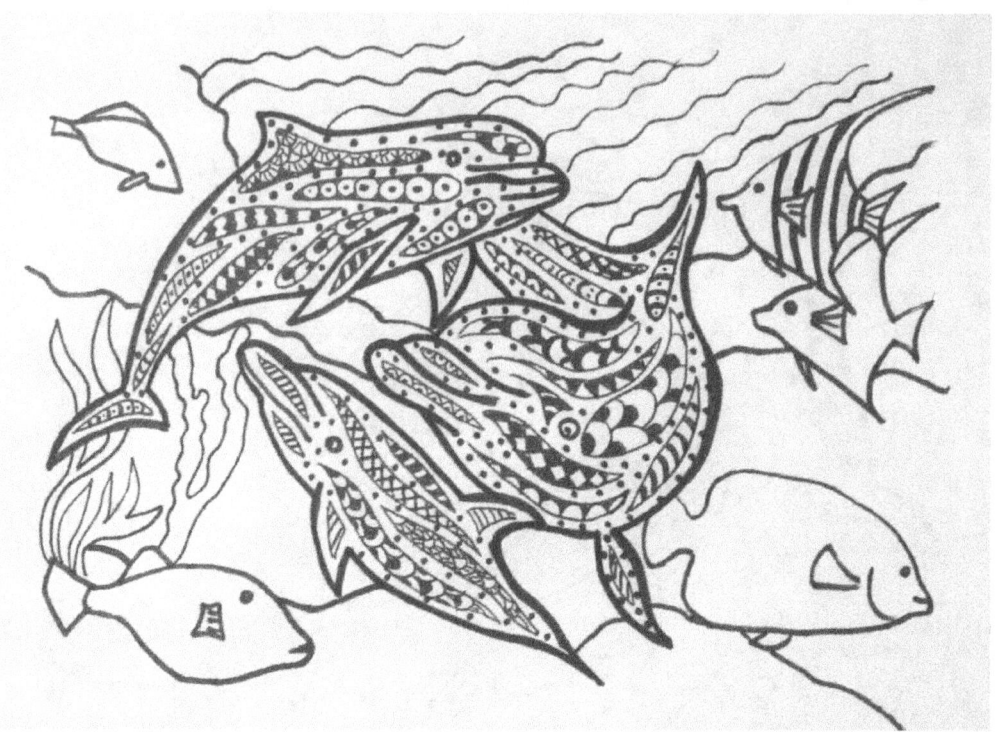

Step 4: This is your last step and you should simply sketch out whatever remains of the fish's balances and after that draw in the paunch of their bodies. Eradicate every one of the rules and shapes that you attracted step one to tidy up your sketch of any undesirable rules.

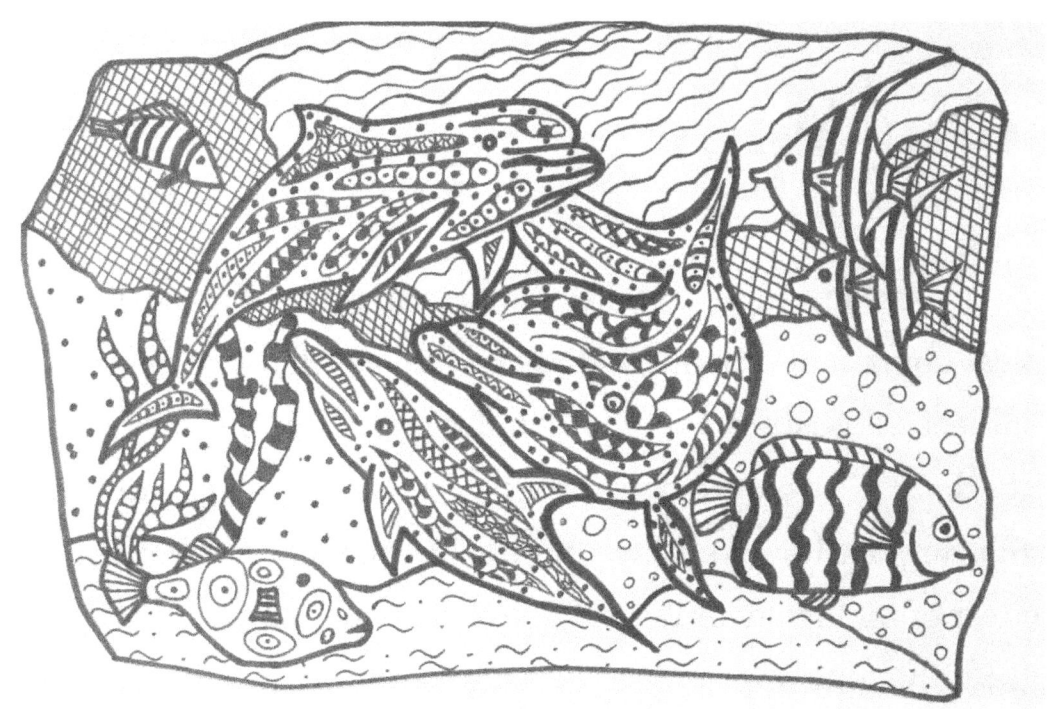

Step 5: At last, you will wind up with three exceptionally adorable fish that you simply figured out how to draw. Color them in any shade you like, and wha-la, you're finished. Trust you all had a great time with this lesson "on the most proficient method to draw fish orderly".

Conclusion

Drawing dream animals takes a few aptitudes that go past the typical domain of drawing in light of the fact that you can't locate a subject to posture for you - unless you live in a captivated timberland! So you are confronted with not just the undertaking of figuring out how to draw you are additionally confronted with the test of taking advantage of your creative ability and after that putting this down on paper. Here are some strong tips that will assist you with envisioning and draw better dream animals.

The most effective method to Tap into your Imagination

Doodling and drawing with a free-form is the most ideal approach to get your innovativeness and creative energy streaming. The procedure to take after is to just draw fast sketches and afterward alter them as things begin. It resembles the following: Draw a generally human formed head then begin to add a body to it however don't intentionally make it a human body, differ your lines and see where it goes. You will be shocked by what happens. Your eye will begin to see things in an alternate manner and you will make some phenomenal animals. These ought to just be snappy sketches and you ought to draw bunches of them - fill the sheet of paper and see where the drawings go. This is an awesome approach to concoct the beginning thought for another dream animal.

Changing the state of existing animals and creatures - Many of the most commonplace dream animals are varieties of recognizable creatures. A Unicorn is a variety of a steed and a Dragon is a variety of a Dinosaur. Consider different animals and doodle their unpleasant shape while concocting varieties. What might a feline look like on the off chance that it had scales rather than hide? Then again what about a Giraffe with short legs?

The Power of Combining Animals - this is an intense approach to make new dream animals and Greek Mythology is stacked with this sort of brute. A Centaur is half man and half stallion; and a mermaid is half lady and half fish. The potential outcomes are inestimable and when you are doodling out thoughts don't constrain yourself to simply upper and lower body mixes. Have a go at consolidating appendages, middles, heads, hands, feet or whatever else that strikes you.

The inventive force of contortion - Often times dream animals are twists of people or different creatures. Think about you're drawing as a chunk of mud that you can form into any shape. Mutilate the arms, legs, middle, head or whatever else. This will harvest some extraordinary results. In the event that you draw a human that is extremely thin with a larger than average head you are making a beeline for something troll like. Also, in the event that you draw a human that is thick and stocky you may be making a beeline for a Troll or Ogre.

Here are a few bizarre approaches to take advantage of your creative ability and make unordinary dream animals. Have a go at making a strange sound then attempt to draw the animal or brute that would make that sound. On the other hand work out a portrayal in words for your monster then attempt to draw it. These two methods bring different parts of your mind into the procedure not simply your dexterity.

The Mechanics of How to Draw Better Fantasy Creatures

Everything identifies with human life structures - If you work on drawing individuals you will show signs of improvement at drawing dream animals. The same fundamental principles of musculature and skeletal understructure apply to every single natural animal - even made up ones. Keep in mind: Skin or hide is something that covers muscles and bones however don't totally conceal it. The bones and muscles appear on the other side. So draw more individuals and your dream animals will move forward.

Draw additionally existing animals - Fantasy animals are quite often varieties of animals and creatures that as of now exist. In the event that you need to draw a mythical serpent you ought to consider and take a gander at pictures of dinosaurs and expansive reptiles. On the off chance that you need to draw a unicorn you ought to utilize a stallion as you're model. Furthermore, there are numerous minor departure from the human structure. On the off chance that you need to draw a diminutive person, a mythical being or a troll you can utilize the human structure as an impeccable beginning stage. The critical thing to recall is that the more stallions you draw the better your unicorns will be and the more dinosaurs you draw the better your winged serpents will be. What's more, the best thing about this is that you can without much of a stretch discover pictures of steeds and dinosaurs to take a gander at while you draw.

Utilize your drawing devices for more expression - When drawing an animal you need to think about its air. Is it a delicate animal or a mean animal? Utilize your pencil in a manner that communicates this. Dull, intense and sharp lines are generally better when drawing irate or terrifying animals and delicate lines are typically better for tender, legendary animals. This is something that is frequently neglected however it is critical. You are utilizing your pencil as a part of a way that goes past simply drawing lines. Furthermore, this applies to an entire range of strategies including short lines, long lines, uneven lines and notwithstanding shading.

Try not to waver to take a gander at and duplicate different people groups work. Precisely taking a gander at other dream work will enhance your work significantly. While doing a duplicate you are compelled to see things you wouldn't regularly see and this is an awesome approach to figure out how to do it without anyone's help. - Just don't guarantee the animal as your own.

Keep a sketch and doodle book and work in it frequently. This is something that works genuine well for me in light of the fact that looking over numerous pages of doodles you have done in the past will regularly motivate new thoughts for drawings of animals.

Drawing dream animals is a testing yet remunerating leisure activity. It has the double advantage of enhancing your capacity to draw while developing your inventiveness and creative energy. With a touch of practice and a comprehension of these essential tips you will be drawing some astonishing dream animals in a matter of seconds by any stretch of the imagination.

A straightforward way to deal with drawing a fish includes getting its key structure right. Two essential shapes can assist you with drawing your ideal fish - An elliptical or square shape for the fish's body and two triangles, one for the head and the other for the tail. Notwithstanding the wide mixed bags of fish, the structure of this water creature continues as before. Pick the sort of fish you might want to draw and improve it further with your inventive creative energy to bring out one of a kind & craved results.

Things You Will Need

1.   Pencil

2.   Paper/Canvas

3.   Colors (discretionary)

4.   Paint Brush (Optional)

Simple & orderly directions to draw a fish

1.   Basic Outline - Once we choose the sort of fish we need to draw, we can make the essential structure of the fish. It includes three essential shapes.

i.   Draw a straight flat line. The line's length will rely on upon the craved measurement of the fish you are drawing.

ii.   Eyes & Tail - At every end of the flat line, make a triangle, guaranteeing the triangles resemble the "play" or 'rewind catches,' both appearing to be identical heading. For this situation, the left most will serve as the fish's substance and the privilege most as its tail.

iii.   Body - The range between the two triangles is the fish's body. Join both the closures making either an elongated shape or a square, contingent upon the mixture of fish you are drawing.

iv.   Erase the supporting and managing lines and obscure the fundamental structure of the fish.

2.   Enhance Features - Put your imaginative capacity in real life while you improve the eyes, balances, tail, & body of the fish. Then again, you can remember these bearings.

i.   Eyes - Draw a circle inside the left triangle ideally in the middle. Presently draw a littler circle inside the external circle and obscure it.

ii.   Mouth of the Fish - From the pointed edge of the triangle, draw a marginally bended line.

iii.   Fins - Along the external line of the fish's body, dispersing out generally, draw two balances on every side.

3.   Shading/Coloring - Shading or coloring draws out the genuine excellence of any drawing or painting.

i.   Eyes - Draw a couple lines under the fish's eyes and obscure the mouth to give it a practical look.

ii.   Body - Draw little semi-circles on the fish body to make it look flaky.

iii.   Fins - Curved or wavy lines can be drawn on the balance and one side of the balance can be shaded darker than the rest.

iv.   Tail - Draw little, fine yet dull & firmly divided lines towards its end.

www.ingramcontent.com/pod-product-compliance
Lightning Source LLC
Chambersburg PA
CBHW080541190526
45169CB00007B/2581